Muscular Poetry IV

KEMO CHEN

ISBN 978-1-956001-37-2 (paperback)
ISBN 978-1-956001-38-9 (eBook)

Copyright © 2021 by Kemo Chen

All rights reserved. No part of this publication may be reproduced, distributed, or transmitted in any form or by any means, including photocopying, recording, or other electronic or mechanical methods without the prior written permission of the publisher.

Printed in the United States of America

Muscular Poetry IV

"There are no great poets, no really bad ones, just poets. All who stitch up that gap in the soul between who we are and who we want to be"

Kemo Chen

Men are more often inclined to bottle up their feelings, critique their every move, over contemplate, and delineate, everything. And it creates a type of emotional and intellectual paralysis that ends creative things before they ever begin, let alone, ensue into being.

The therapy of creativity is stymied. What might provide solace is silenced.

Men, at times tormented, or worse in denial of pent up desires, seek therapies, to not much avail. Freud provides insights of times past; Adler of wills to power and other foreign constructs; Jung challenges our masks and ideas about self; Maslow claims it's about actualization; cognitive behavioral dudes offer up bromides and awareness exercises; and, then there are serotonin uptake inhibitors, LSD, and cannabis derivatives.

But, we know, the answers are inside. The trick is to access them. And writing can help get you to them, if you can just sit, alone, in front of a blank page, and knock out a sentence or two. And, overtime, it pours out of you.

Poetry releases the furies, the unshed tears, the arguments with unspent anger, everything unexpressed, expressed. Poetry is a big damn sneeze, about to happen, held back for years; that orgasm you once longed for, waiting to return with any frequency again.

And it's neither good nor awful. As you will see within, this volume, it is about raw emotion, genuine feelings. Some of it you will share, reject others, outright scream at some, and wonder how come, this nut wrote this anyway.

No matter. It's just honest stuff, what I have observed, wondered about, lost sleep over, or cried for on really bad days, and those nights alone, just me, the feelings and a dawn about to come.

I'm an unknown, trying to share something, in the hope it motivates you to write a poem or two, from time to time. I hope it gives you the permission to say, "screw it, this is on my mind", and you write your own volumes, or stuff a single poem into your back pocket after or before work. Don't judge it. In fact, stop judging so much. Open up, relax, and be the man within.

Kemo Chen 2021

The Poems

(Suggested Dose: Three to Five a Session,
Reading Time One to Three Minutes)

My Pop Tarts are Always Broken 1
Everyone has an Achilles Heel 4
Look What You Have Done to Me 6
Immortality Carved in a Tree..9
Batter Up 11
Disagreeables..13
Gregg or Pitman? 16
Remember Betar 18
The Quiet Mind 20
No Bridge Too Far..22
77 Lives Saved and One More 24
Galileo's Finger...26
Nothing Left 29
The Most Vile of Men...31
W.O.A.T...33
August Humility 36
Capone Played the Banjo 39
Morning Wood 41
Where Did I Put My Soul 43

There are No Witches	46
The Last Time I Saw Joe	49
Say What's on Your Mind	52
At the Checkout Counter	55
Stubborn Nation	58
SpeedBalling at Chateau Marmont	60
What Side of the Bed Did You Sleep On	63
One Legged Wake Up Call	65
What Do the Damn Critics Know	67
Moonglow	69
Just Another Day at El Pollo Loco	71
Nietzsche on the Boardwalk	73
Letting Go	75
The Jew in The Middle; Circa 5780	78
I See Her Face	81
How Men Die	84
The NFL Played Again	88
Drinking Ants at 5:45	90
Gross Hematuria	93
No Time To Dream	96
Swimming to Galilee	98
Pipe Dreams	100
The Glory that was Rome	103
Loosen the Grip on the Rudder	106
Wonder What It Is Like Struggling with Fame	108
Leopard Bikini Under a Harvest Moon	111
October night	113
You were Happy When	114

He Just Wanted to Get Laid	117
You Need to Get Out and Date	120
The Belt in the Box	122
Where Did All The Strippers Go	124
A Little Woman With a Green Wig	126
Even the Soap Dish Must be Cleaned	129
The Religion of Woke	131
Goodbye Columbus	133
And the Dawn Comes	135
No Miracle on 34th Street	137
Petty Misery	139
On The Drive Back to the 475 Square	141
Speaking Freely while Being Strangled	143
Where Have All the Axes Gone	145
No More Dalai Lama's	147
The Bastards Cut The Eucalyptus Tree	150
Eight Dollars and Some Change	152
There Will Always Be Critics	154
Send Me a Muse	156
King Tide Come and Low Tide Go Me With the Treacherous Undertow	158
526 in '54	159
Beating the Crap Out of America	161
Too Many UGB's	164
Saving George Bailey	167
The Man in the Next Seat to Wilmington	169
Moon Over the Bay	172
The Stop Sign is 100 Yards Away	174
Gotta Stay Ahead of the Wave	177

Warm Winter Wind	180
No Argument Here	182
Waiting on a Sidewalk	184
In an Archway on 72nd at 10: 50	186
So Who Are You Dating	188
You Are Not Your Pain	191
The Commute	193
Clear Headed	196
Agent 488- Who Are You?	199
Never Play In Any Reindeer Games	202
What You Miss	204
Will I Run Fast Again	207
Curbside Moral Dilemmas	210
Horseradish Memories	213
Knucksie	215
The Pioneer Takes the Arrows	217
58,220 KIA	219
The Ball Drops with No one There	221
Defacing Abe	223
All the Guys I Know	225
Her Fingers on His Lips	227
Intersectional Literature	229
Tranquility Lost	231
Shift the Damn Gestalt	233
The Facel Vega Hits a Tree	235
The Jockey and the Showgirl	237
Where did all the Vices Go?	240
Hang Mike Pence	243

Sweet N' Low	246
They're Dying in the ICU's	249
Nobody Cares What I Think	252
Would They Banish Christ on Twitter	255
Worn Out from the Inside Out	258
Just Leave Me the hell alone	260
Mortified	263
The Rape of Xinjiang	266
On Any Given Super Bowl Sunday	269
That Vacuum Cleaner	273
Exiled	275
Now Pauly is Gone	278
No Valentine to Open	281
Stabbed Twenty Three times on a Mild March Day	284
Can Hack the Day but not the Night	287
Zephyr in the Kitchen	289
Falling in Love Again	292
Whatever Became of Red Levine	295
A Still Point in a Turning World	297
Sense Memory – Cold	299
Enlarged or Reduced by Life	302
Say Goodbye to Patsy's	305
Before the Dogs Awake	308
Can't make that Spare	310
Just Then Awareness Comes	313
Street Fights	316
Drive Thru Epiphany	318
The Torch of Truth	321

Non Fungible Tokens 324
Marie Made it to 92 326
Where are You? 329
Say Goodbye to Western Civilization 332
Ode to Spring 334
You Don't Need a Fire to Burn a Book 337
Get Over It 341
Defenestration 344
All My References Are Dead 346
Why Did He Kill Them 348
Welcome to Potemkin Village 351
Hey, There is a Soul in There 353
The Hand of Pluto 355
On The Razor Wire 357
Easter Sunrise 359
Filling the Holes 362
What the Trail Knows 365
One Swallow to Forget Everything 367
The Only Answer is 370
Out of Nothing 373
Just One Day is All 375
If Life Could Only Be Like Basketball 377
What The Crow Knows 379
Is This Really Love? 381
Wind of Change 384
Finally 387
The Perfect Day Illusion 390
When Will Love Return 393

Panel 16E- Line 94	397
The Only Honest Writing	400
A Walk in the Rain	403
Every 17 Years	405
4 May	408
Accusations Everywhere	411
A Cider Jar in a Beer Cooler	414
The Orange Sun Sinks	417
Nazi's of a Different Hue	419
Where Has My Libido Gone?	422
Weary of Rebuke	424
Photos in an Arcade Booth	427
Cowboys and Country Music	430
Mercury in Retrograde	433
Neither Aaron nor Rose	436
Fruit Mix in Extra Light Syrup	439
Henry Ford Rolling in the Grave	441
There is a Fear	444
One August Day Outside Mexico City	447
Admonitions	450
Batting Cage	453
Last of the Liberators	455
Last Night in Rancho Mirage	458
Going 80 on a Desert Road	461
Al is Not Al Anymore	464
Ultimate Cancel Culture Revenge	467
Grey Morning	469
Tools	471

Don't Mess with the Gestalt 474
The Turandot Three 476
Anger Comes 479
Red Bikini, Three Legged Dog 482
Who Stole the Melting Pot...484
End Talks 487
The Desperate Man..489
Who Do You Think You Are 491

My Pop Tarts are Always Broken

Got my working papers at 15
Took two buses to get to work
Walked a mile or so to empty trash cans
at a public golf course, and dispense
Black and white milk shakes at the
soda bar
gulped an overcooked burger at the grill
and saved cold fries for the buses home
brought a clean shirt, so I didn't smell
like the garbage man

then in space age foil, there appeared
something called a pop tart
that my Mom put into a pre war toaster
and served it up to Dad before he commuted off
to his job at Sears
not fancy, no glaze,
I took to put them in my pants to
Bus to work and ate it usually along the way
Cold of course
And always crumbled, never as planned,
Since I was not a toaster fan
Old Frank Kellogg's brand

Nothing more than something thin
Spread between the thin pastry
But it was durable and seemingly fresh
Ate them frosted and not through college
degrees, advanced studies, teaching,
grown up professions, marriage, children,
divorce and more

an unusual constant as I marched quietly
towards the abyss
on trains to Manhattan, the LIE, green line to
Boston City Hall, clogged along the 405
The Pop Tart was, invariably by my side
Cold
Crushed
symbolic of a rather ordinary, disoriented life

dropped them after 9/11
millions over Afghanistan
shipped freshly to continents
even though they burned in toasters
when unwatched, became the brunt of
bad jokes and barroom humor for the
Comedy Club lot

a staple
for men after adolescent memories
who pocketed them, recall shoving them in
glove compartments, as they romanced
Fern, hoping to parlay second to third base

And, somehow, no matter what
The Pop Tart, I had was always
Crushed
Whether omen or talisman an indicator
of how random anything can be,
represent or symbolize
and the fresh and tasty things can
still crumble, regularly, right before your
eyes......

Everyone has an Achilles Heel

Even the heels of history
The preeminent louses
Loud mouthed, bastards who contend
They alone own the truth of things
Unable to see their conceit
Admiring their bald heads, fat lips, and
Thick hands, and their short fingers grasping
At flesh and fowl with equal abandon

They can scare the morality out of men
Afraid to stand up to them
When Joe McCarthy ordered steak he wanted
It "cremated"
Got what he asked, no one said why, or no
To this consummate pig from long ago

He ate steak, and anything else he could swallow
To fill the hole in his blackened soul, the color of his
Prime rib and T bone
While the witnesses shuttered to be banned
Labeled a commie man
He drank from a flask of whiskey
Ate his way to clogged arteries

And each night poured enough bicarbonate
Into his gut, to calm it down

Before, his time expired on his reign of
Self- aggrandizement,
before they called,
out, "Senator do you have no sense of dignity"
before Murrow and Friendly called him out as
a fraud and demagogue

he would swallow a half a pound of butter
each morning, to ward off the effect of the booze on
his decaying gut
he lived an agony of his own
consumptive making

he was not dipped by the Gods
in magical, protective waters,
no mother to hold him by his heel
he could not shut his mouth
consider what went in or came out
attempting to prove he existed by
stuffing himself to excess and
believing his lies
and destroying everything around him
and never thinking he would
eventually destroy himself

Look What You Have Done to Me

Nothing is what is was once
anymore
May gray fades, June gloom comes and
Goes
Wild fires come anytime, and everywhere
From hamlet and horse lands blazing through
City streets and shopping malls

A moonlit July night over the bay
Blocked by a deep marine level
A cold grey forces shoulders and cheeks to
merge, by fires built of chopped up
palettes

A circle of young women in sweatshirts
proclaiming their intellectual prowess and parents
worth
Harvard, Yale, Northwestern, Michigan,
And a redhead from San Diego State, hip to hip
With the brunette from UCLA
Legs and bikini bottoms
Contemplating the larger life concerns

"So, I thought, I want to be married and have kids, you know
How do I set distinct goals to get to that result"
Yale mentioned to them all

Two couples lay entwined
By the abandoned volleyball court
Hip hop tunes served as backbeat
For serpentine tongues tangled
In the foreplay of the moment
presaging each sinking into the other
before dawn

Benny sorted through his clothes
Pulled out his blanket, at his night spot
by the woman's rowing club
lit his reefer, took long puffs
and blew grey rings into the darkening night
lay on his back, and rested his 260 pounds
down for the night

got back to my 460 square
about to eat a defrosted something
and some green tea
Elaine is screaming right below me
"Fuck you, fuck you, you lying fucking bastard"
The unnamed jerk, responds in a stupor
"yeah Elaine, well, yeah, so, so,"
"nothing, you bitch, nothing, you gave me"
"no shit, not even that, I'm gone"
Elaine

"fuck you, look what you've done to me"

They walk away into the full moon night
grumbling, lost, out of the reach of reason
and compassion

people howl at the moon in July
by the bay
whether you can see it
or not.

Immortality Carved in a Tree

It once probably occurred to me
To carve my initials in a tree
A signal it would be to imagined
Eternity
That I was here that day and mattered
Some to somebody, or just to me

Markings flourished on bark even on trees
Outside of parks, trees along concrete
Sidewalks, barely shading boys sitting on curbs
After a stickball contest
Sweat soaked shirts, and broad smiles
Managed to unleash a pocketknife
And carve J.B. '67
Duke '56
Cos '62

Declarations of existence
I am here the carvings say
Years pass, who they became or
Were faded by time and circumstance
Leaving only these healed scars
Markers of a young man's being

Caught in prime, unlike the etched stone
That bears his full name and place
In a suburban plot, beneath a well manicured
green space where people come to cry

a jade green river runs towards the city
along banks where lovers walked, groped,
proclaiming eternal bliss
hearts are found crafted by a man determined
to etch his devotion and dedication to the woman
to whom he is bound
large or small the message
the same
J.K. plus S. D.
Bob plus Kay
D and J
Do they last as long together as what the knife
Proclaimed on that day?

There will always be a Kilroy
Saying I was here
Wondering now what I have etched on my
cosmic tree, time to put away the knife

Batter Up

What would Babe and Lou say
Would Dimaggio and Mantle even play
to a ballpark empty for the next sixty days?

No taunts, no cups of beer tossed
their way
No Dodger dogs, knockwursts, peanut bags
Flying over heads, caught by boys waiting
To become men

The summer sun warms empty rows
after row
Where fans sat shirtless to get that
admired tan, and catch a line drive in
their bare hand

no one there to protest and howl
an umpires bad call
cheer on Durocher or Billy Martin
as they kick the dirt on the umps
shined shoes
only the voices, behind fabric, of the
boys of summer, playing for TV, cash money,

holding onto their contractual obligations
fearing the owners retaliation

lousy days of play
nostalgia still to be made
unlike milestones of the game
from Robinson, Ruth, Maris,
Ripken, Mays, and the others in
Cooperstown

What will be remembered here
Of men who played in a diseased year
To seats unfilled, the quiet of fear
The strikes still came, the curves did not abate
As men put it all away to
play, the game they loved

Disagreeables

Kings demanded it
Tyrants beat you into it
Dictators and demagogues convinced
With a stranglehold on truth
And words that made it appear they
Carried about you

Agreement on all things they
said was true, with no other hue
And if you dared cry out, any of it was a lie
You could surely be crushed, exiled or
eliminated on any given day
Turn the righteous mob on you
Strip you naked of your point of view
And beat it out of you

So they agree,
Do you
America started in 1691 not 1776
Disagree
All white folks are racist
Disagree
America is systemically racist

Disagree
Cops kill more black folks than anyone
Factually, in error, and disagree
Defund the police
Disagree, it hurts the people that need them most
Prisons are filled with felons, unfairly there, who should be set free
Disagree
All blacks should receive reparations
Disagree, there must be a better plan
Socialism is the answer
Disagree, it has never worked anywhere
Raise the taxes on those who can pay\
Leave the rest of us alone
Disagree, it is the few that pay anyway
Throw away the Judeo- Christian values
Wipe away Western Civilization
Alter history to say it's the story of oppression
And victimization of black and brown
Coerce anyone who disagrees
To shut up or pay the price
of riots through the nights

Marx was a loafer, who misread the future
Miserably
Lenin, Stalin, Mao knew best that anyone who
disagreed had to be destroyed
as they murdered millions in the quest to
guarantee one view, and agreement on everything

Dare express a view that you are not racist
nor in the USA, or that cops are saviors, and not the
punks who riot from Portland to Boston,
proclaiming a single point of view
that is arguably untrue
and if you dare cite facts and disagree
vandalism will ensue, not just to trash your store
but take your job, troll your kids,
thoroughly ostracize
you
they want to outlaw strangeholds on perps that cops
encounter
but have firmly placed your head inside a carotid hold
so you cannot breath or speak
squeezing disagreement, once full throated into but a murmur
believing they are righteous, when they are not

Gregg or Pitman?

As far back as one man had something to utter
that he wanted written down, on papyrus, parchment,
sheep skin or even etched in stone
scribes appeared with stylus, pen, and chisel
man to man
Marcus Tullius Tiro in 4B CE sat at Cicero's feet
The first modern secretary,perhaps, with his
Tironian notes
That set the stage for

Actual secretaries, I love Lucy types, struggling through
shorthand, as William Holden dictates,
as if he cared about the letter
rather than her legs
offices filled with them
attentive, engaging, on the make for some,
gatekeepers, protectors, and deflectors
you could get somewhere,fast with the right one

when you'd interview one you'd ask
Gregg or Pitman?
Sir Issac Pitman in 1837
Laid down his squiggles

John Gregg in 1888 made his quicker
Fathers of the steno pool
Making brachygraphy into
Good ole' shorthand

Can't find a steno pad now
Nor a long legged siren who
Still wants to play
All that interchange, flirting,
gone to back in the day

rather have Lucy than Alexi
a tall brunette with a great smile than
an I phone
and someone who fooled you to believe
she actually cared about you
at least from 9- 5.

Remember Betar

Streets become rivers of blood
No My Lai nor Nuremberg here
Back in Rome they rejoice
That their legions
Figured out a way to behead an infant
Pile up their frozen faces, take out
300 brains
pulse beside their skulls in the summer heat
smashed on a sharp rock
all of children
bodies burned, dismembered,
mutilated by sword or spear
left to rot
heads without bodies, bodies without limbs
everywhere dead Jews, only Jews

who dared for three years to defy
Hadrian and more Rome
Even after the Temple was razed
Jerusalem flattened, and renamed
A champion came
Bar Kokhba by name
With a biblical claim

That could only unnerve and inflame
The Emperor, who wanted the Jews
To just go away

Might overcomes righteousness
Resolve and grit
Legions adept at annihilation overtake
rebels no matter how godly their cause
superior force overtakes even the most worthy
of plans
destiny decides and good men die

summer of 135
the legions breakthrough Betar
kill them all, but one
and a half a million more
to make sure no Jew will raise
a hand again or dream of a homeland
Hadrian waited through the clear night
star gazed until
Bar Kokhba's head came to his tent on
a spear
"they will not soon forget this"
And they did not
1,813 years to Israeli state
millions dead from pogroms, inquisitions, holocaust
remembering, screams of children, over the sound of skulls, crushed on
a boulder on a street in Betar, 4 August 135 CE

The Quiet Mind

Do men ever do nothing anymore
Just sit on a couch, with nothing more
than a thought rolling through their
brain
a place between things, a Sabbath time
where devices are off
screens blank, no one else around
no incursions, diversions, worries
shoved away for a moment or two
each day

that's not to say that there is not
Zen in motion
when you cross into a zone
and never want it to end
as the moment elongates
envelopes and overtakes everything
and there is nothing else
for just then

can epiphanies arrive
in a cluttered life, where there is
never really any play?

Thumbs in constant motion straining to
say something, every damn moment of every
day
eyes down, chin in unraised chest
shoulders hunched and frozen, never back
and straight and bold
voices silenced by electronic masters
who have figured out to communicate and
mute all of us

a contemplative can be seized
by only taking the time to have it
men need a pause, allowance to be at ease
so some idea might be incubated, problem cracked open
away from the fray, the taunts, concerns, arguments,
and all petty miseries
that hold us back from a unforeseen leap towards
resolution and illumination on any other thing
the noise,the blue light is strangling whatever might
evolve, in a space between answering her text and the PGA
tournament on TV

No Bridge Too Far

A horse pulls a hearse
across an Alabama bridge
quiet now
red rose petals each symbols of
a drop of blood, he shed
standing for rights, God given,
inalienable, it is said, but denied
a half century ago
as troopers cracked his head
beating young, John Lewis to the
ground under
the Edmund Pettus Bridge

by any measure, in any time,
anywhere, even here in Selma
this man Pettus was not just of his
time, but for any time, far from worthy
of praise
the litany of hate well known, even when
the bridge was named
traitor to the USA, leader of the KKK
Senator back in the day who voted to
keep, a generation of John Lewis' at bay

Lewis came to be jailed that day
committed to not raise a hand
in his backpack, a book of a Trappist monk,
and another from a political pundit, a toothbrush and paste,
an apple
not the wherewithal of a terrorist or a commie
no TNT or acid to toss at his tormentors

Now come the "erase history" mob
From West LA and the Upper East Side
resurrect the bridge with Lewis' name
they scream with their thumbs and phones

but wise John knew that
"you can change the name, but you cannot change
the facts of history"
he would often proclaim to those still angry for him
there is more to do, and to move along
there are some odious symbols of the past
that must remain from Auschwitz to Selma
Arbeit Macht Frei to the Edmund Pettus Bridge
so we never forget what happened here

77 Lives Saved and One More

Looking back over time
it is easy enough to spot destiny
as the moments evolve not so much
as it was sitting in a high lifeguard chair
overlooking that Rock River that ran
through Lowell Park
for one 15 year old, named Dutch in Dixon, Illinois

over seven summers, this tall handsome boy
turned man, with an easy brilliant smile,
quietly saved lives
had a log by his stuff that he notched
for each life, 77 when he took his towel
and called it quits

learned to do his job
be accommodating, dived in for a man's lost
teeth, pulled out a few dogs
and when he wanted folks out of the water
he'd throw stones into the water and shout
"river rats.. river rats…"

And watch them run for their lives to shore

Early years often reveal what a man will
become, naturally, no matter what else pulls him
away from himself

On a 1969, June day in Sacramento by the
pool at the Governor's mansion, 7 year old
Alicia Berry lost her grip on the pools edge
And went under
Dutch caught her in his lifeguard eyes, counted to
Ten, and when she did not bob up, he jumped in
Clothes and all and pulled her out
Number 78, log long gone to notch
But it was as vital to him as the days on
Rock River

A man with a purpose, cellular and ingrained
to rescue, for no acclaim, only to sustain who he was
saving souls that you could notch on a log or in memory
until it was about saving a nation and even the world,
until he took his towel and went home, again.

Galileo's Finger

What do men great and not
Leave behind
To remember them by
a table of Maplewood, a garden of succulents,
a box of ancient tools, a worn Yankee hat
something signed by someone thought famous?

Or is it just what they thought
mined intellectually, observed majestically
And then passed along, accepted finally by the
mainstream that made them swim upstream
endlessly

Galileo Galilei discovered moons
toppled Ptolemy's and Aristotle's accepted
notions that Earth was the center of it all
Copernicus knew better the Inquisitor's
heard him say in 1616, and took them some years
to convict him for being "heliocentric" which was
heresy, the grand inquisitor, Vincenzo Maculani
would come to say

No matter, he proved
Jupiter had moons
old Aristotle had gravity wrong
even as David Scott showed again in
1971, in that perfect vacuum
250,000 miles away
when a hammer drops with a falcon
feather, they fall at the same rate

they forced him to recant what he certainly
knew about the Earth and the Sun too
paid for his point of view
coerced to comply in June 1632
exiled to house arrest, until he
crumbled under the weight of the big lie
8 January 1642

Afraid to bury him somewhere sublime
They put him in a pit, only to be reclaimed
95 years later, when an enthusiastic grave robber
named Anton Gori, broke off his middle finger,
thumb and forefinger and pulled three teeth out
of his skull

overlooking the banks of the Arno
a glass dome holds that middle finger
pointing towards his studied heavens
along with the others digits and one tooth
now
a reminder of a man

and his genius DNA
reduced to a mere
bony display

leaving the universal salute of
distain
a single finger to proclaim
the triumph of genius over
inquisition, intolerance
and the shame of renouncing
what you know is true to
stay alive

Nothing Left

A concrete prairie rolls flat and hard
behind the Walmart
a line of dumpsters define the perimeter
a single light casts a spotlight on
what's left of a man on all fours
sifting through a garbage bag he has
eviscerated to find a meal

light bulbs and underwear brought me here
and I see him in my rearview
pause
as he crawls to whatever food he found
so gaunt, in actual rags, a figure from
a monstrously long Hugo novel
but not 1870, now

what might it be that puts him here
forces and fate most say
booze, drugs, perhaps, but more likely
what we used to call insane
lucidity,might come and fade
meds bring clarity some of the day
until the reality of it all, seeps in

and no man wants to live conscious of that
anyway
so throw the meds away, dissolve reality in
a bottle, or send it to oblivion with a needle
caught in some vein, between your toes

and yet
organisms don't give up
they carry on, until
their life cycle is done,
he is not finished
his something is survival
which is noble and enough
tonight

I drive away inspired
oddly, to stop the constant whine
and get about living with my time
before I have really have nothing left

The Most Vile of Men

Washington had slaves
123 they say some freed by Martha
on his judgment day
Jefferson had hundreds more
fathered some with a 14 year old
he took a likin to

Teddy killed trophies of every type
and kind
thought the "white race" was designed
to lead the world for all time
for what he preserved, conserved, busted up
and energized
he was a racist for sure deep inside

their greatness ensued not from
being of their narrow mind
but that they transcended it for
grander causes they left behind

What you leave behind is enshrined
who you were, no matter how vile
not matter?

Rushmore exists revealed in stone
by a KKK devotee
a Jew baiter worthy of Mengele
avowed racist
this Gutzon Borglum
who left behind a majestic
work of public art
even as despised in his day as now

Hard to find an artist as despicable
and as monumentally hateful
yet, what is served other than
impulsive revenge
leaving a pile of dust, returns no freedom,
reclaims no Native land
his name will be forgotten, as master builders
of the ages
and the faces that remain remind us
that we must always rise above the times
offer more, embrace our differences,
and repair a world broken by others hate

W.O.A.T

It can't be so bad out there
even as tolerance is wounded
dissent beaten into compliance
everyone who is not on their side
to wipe out history, art and any
memory of Western civilization
coerced into silence

so you adopt the Panglossian
manner, that this is the best of times
not worst of all times
that your friends all say
forgetting that Pangloss
had reason for his outlook
surviving being hanged, being carved up
assumed dead, and sewn up and sent on his way

rope and knife do not touch us all
but bruises to thought, liberty, and
free speech, can damage us more, indelibly

modern sperm swim in corkscrews towards fertile eggs
nothing is linear anymore
a museum called for a century The Museum of Man
amended it, to be of "US". A deft emasculation of nameplate
but exhibits altered to proclaim, men are in retreat

Male curator of fine art is thrown to
the curb, ousted because
he dared say
"I will continue to curate for Picasso, Pollack,
Braque, Van Gogh, Calder, and,that old scoundrel,
Matisse"
The board of wokers, found it insane that he would
Want the art of "white" men to be portrayed
Enough of that we already have on our wall
They did say

Not the worst of times, Mr. Dickens
Even as three dozen black Seattle protestors
march up a suburban street
screaming to the huddled homeowners
"we want your fucking homes. They belong to
You can't shit us, you motherfuckers. This is our land
Before you white fucks bought it up. We are coming for you
Fuck you gentrifying fucks. Give it up whitey"

Just another day in the best of all possible worlds?
The wokers sleep well, their targets afraid to say anything
Lock their doors, and load their pistols
The times they are a changing goes the

folk song,
no Age of Aquarius, there is a turn in the road
to the place where fire, and fury reside
on the way to Hell

August Humility

Richard Alpert went to India
after dropping LSD, with Timothy Leary
to find his way
rubbed up to a Hindu guru
and became Baba Ram Dass
proclaiming Buddhist thought
the "right way"

down an eight fold path
with simple practices every day
to be here, now, awake to every
moment, since what was is over
and what is next, who is to say?

And if you are troubled
overwhelmed, suffering
throw off the embellishments of
your ego and status, and return
to being nothing more than
a humble sentient being that
can chop wood and can carry water
just one more day

Big Danny never heard of Ram Dass
or that life is suffering
he sells cars off the lot of his dealership off the 405,
and always has a
smile,
his phone is always active
and he never seems to stop
except for his rock band, where he channels
Metallica's, James Hetfield
or his girlfriend Julie, all Vegas showgirl
of her

Never had a word of doubt
a decline in energy
sees himself as capable of everything
except this thing called
humility

its 105 in the Valley
I am on my hands and knees
Scrubbing the bathroom, kitchen floors
Sweat in my eyeballs
August humidity descends
Dampness wrings the aspirations out of me
Wiping the tub, toilet Mr. Clean,
Clean
Hard to be a master of the universe or
think you are
with Clorox in your nostrils and a rag in
your left hand

No guru needed
No trip to his distant ashram
humility comes when it does
to guys like me
while Big Danny and Julie
lower the rag top of the sky blue
Bentley, leave the more showy
Black Rolls in the garage
and drive up PCH to Malibu

Capone Played the Banjo

In a prison band,
The Rock Islanders they were called
Al asked the warden if it would
Be alright
To play the banjo, Mae sent him to
Pass away the time
In this Alcatraz cell

After all, convict 85, convinced the screws
He wasn't in for the prostitution, the
rackets, booze, or the rub outs he
had notched with Nitti and the mob
it was for tax evasion, hardly worth
the time

Al lived large, with pools, verandas
Cooks and chefs
The banjo was a connection
To distract him from his 5 by 9
Cell 133 in B block
He played with average dexterity
Al now sick as much well
His life creating hell for others

was providing payback now
but strum along he did, and
smiled, not cracking wise
or shouting out with his distinctive
Brooklyn whine

Still he was Capone
So he was treated ok
Got a carpet, and a radio
And the guards would sit and talk

Eventually Mae got him a
Tenor mandola, with a somewhat
sweeter sound
so he could forget the discordant screams from
Scalise, Anselmi, Giunta
Who thought they were at a dinner to honor
them
when Al beat their heads, bat in hand
the syncopated rhythm of bullets,into their flesh calmed him.

Morning Wood

Manhood comes at dawn
and in the deepest part of night
at first startles then confirms
that the boy you have been is
leaving this bed, just a few yards
away from where your parents
sleep and intertwine

it becomes a secret in the house
that remains unspoken through
all of your years
offered only to other boys of your clan
to prove your passage from boy to man

you rise hardened
beneath the covers
blood flows through you
signaling puberty in essence
pulsating for attention
when given offers a Darwinian
release worthy of Adam to Eve

then there are dreams that come

willed and not, because all you can
do is dream of couplings seemingly
millions of years away
and for years you awaken wet
fluids finding their way outward
an organisms reproductive forces
searching for
its targets

decades pass, enough rises and falls
insertions, ejaculations, fertilizations
awakening mostly to nothing more
than a worn prostrates call to release
a full bladder
and when the rare wood returns
to smile and honor it
recalling the milestone it was once
when you were about to be a man
and leave boyhood things behind

Where Did I Put My Soul

Live your best life
Take care of yourself and your fellow man
Be kind rather than mean
Help others when you can
Be responsible to your progeny
Treat everyone the same, throw prejudice
away
overcome your flaws, find some purpose
they all say
your consciousness is of your making
as long as you are free to say
whatever the hell you want

yet, that's not enough, never was
as far back as we can tell
there is this notion of another place
eternal where, this core of us will
eventually dwell
before the Egyptians, the kings of Babylon,
cavemen put their corpses away
ready it seems to be reborn
in another way

Were men so certain that this life
was so flawed that they needed another
shot to join soul and body
or
was the majesty and miracle so clear
that it would be wasted with just the time
allotted by a master force who was watching

an explosion of places to go
to retrieve your soul
heaven, of course, but not directly
many netherworlds, Hades, a stop
in Purgatory, a long list of gatekeepers
from three headed dogs, to prophets at the
Pearly Gate

Some souls get their own planets
Become angels
others await a Messiah who when he returns
puts body and soul back together
then others, simply say what you are and were
lives on in others day to day

John you know makes it clear
Believe in him and you go far
eternally, if not when He returns
you're gone, no matter how noble
you may have been, only believers
go on, regardless of how they sinned

too damn complex
in those last moments before you're gone
to figure out if this soul of yours
is headed anywhere, there are enough
destinations out there, trillions of stars and
places to stay 100 billion light years away

running out of time to join up and get
on a religious soul train
just kick around and continue to do what's
seems right, until it all turns into one damn
dark night

and hope my soul knows the way, to the light.

There are No Witches Hang Them Anyway

Bizarre it seems to reflect that
14 women dangled from a rope
along with 5 old men
back in 1692 and '93
Thirty declared guilty in ole'
Salem
200 more accused of
something that just was never true
no matter what the hysterical Puritans
might say, was a lie then, and today

tragedy ensued as scared and stupid
people claimed, that witches were out
to claim the devil's due in 1692

Wise men at the apex of the food chain
elders of the time
did not stomp out the injustice
Increase Mather in his prime ruling
Harvard so sublime
Cotton who at 12 entered his father's school
Had a Harvard degree, and was a Boston

Brahman for sure, stood bye, and let them die
Knowing inside the should not abide
But let the lie just grow, until it became
The way, if never true

The nooses are knotted, yet, today
as Black Lives Matter banshees scream that
America is only a racist scheme
everything a systemic brew of white privilege
economic exclusion, and pure hate

truth does not matter
cops are of all races, rarely shoot anybody
big towns have black mayors, and chiefs
racism surely exists but not systemically
it is a lie, that fuels a movement towards
progressive socialism, less cops and more
crime

all movements based on fundamental falsehoods
become more virulent, putrid, and destructive
whether it hunting for witches, Jews, intellectuals,
or just anyone who dares to disagree with a faulty
premise that grows into a cancerous ideology, theme,
or notion, where sane people die, under the wrath
of the tormentors

fear gives them power
truth dies
people hang in public squares

are humiliated in front of
committees, or have their heads
kicked in on a Portland street

and the wise men watch and smile
with a studied nonchalance
wanting so to believe what is wrong
is right, so they can be left alone to
study, contemplate, and pontificate
as innocence dies at the end of a rope,
in an oven, or the internet

The Last Time I Saw Joe

Holmes strolled by the blackjack table
at Caesars
not that popular as most champs
still he shook hands, and barely smiled
Dundee threw in the towel for Ali
After the tenth round
In a fight where no opening bell
should ever have tolled

Two men at Caesars knew of mismatches
after being the "greatest of all time"
Ali walked gamely, unsteady through the
Casino floor
To cheers

And in the back lot
Where the fighters trained
A man is wheeled in
And I can see the familiar face
Even at 66 of the "brown bomber"
Joe Louis
waves at the handful of us
fighters give him kisses and

brush his face with their gloves and
wrapped hands
the smell of sweat rising and rosin
fills nostrils

a bell rings
of an ice cream truck
a busload of school kids come in
and the most elegant fighter of his time
gives every child a cone, and a smile
the memory of his last fight with
Marciano, distant

A display of humility
Without being humbled
A spirit transcendent still
Children cannot know, but will remember
this

The world will never see him again
Holmes/Berbick is the last rounds he will
ever see, a heart attack is
the final punch
Max Schmeling puts up the cash to
bury his old friend, who knocked him
cold in one round in '38

record books, old films
cannot capture the essence of a man
what he does after the ring does that

ice cream cones and a warm smile
from a wheelchair also
makes a champ for all time

Say What's on Your Mind

Never contemplated being silent
afraid to speak up, articulate even
pontificate what struck me at the
time
aware that there were times to say nothing
so as not to hurt, excite or disturb someone
close,even loved, at least from my
side

not the mundane protestations
of life gone awry, the squabbles that
became negotiations, at various intensities
eventually exploding into impasses that
could never be sealed
across our divides

speech once guaranteed
against injustice, unfairness,
the mighty who were wrong, defending
the meek, speaking truth, no matter what
at your peril, all the time
and moving forward with a million others
by your side

cool glass of water on a humid August day
saying what is on your mind, a constitutional
refreshment that cost you nothing

not today, my voice silenced
afraid to say that's wrong or
here is my point of view, coerced away
as out of touch and tune with the narrative
of the day

Too many grievances for me
all complaint and agony
we are all racists, display sexism,
bigotry, violent, warmongers, xenophobic
enmity to immigrants, legal or not,
opportunity suppressed due to elitism, and
imbedded hate rising from hate of others,
including an inborn, immutable trait of
discrimination by color and race

so I have resolved to speak still
no matter how ill regarded
there is courage needed now
backbone, no matter consequence
or derision

the truth may not emerge
be beaten back to silence
but why not say what is own your
mind anyway

there may be someone to listen
or reject and vilify it all
easy enough choice for a lonely
man attached to nothing but his
sense of right and wrong

what of you with something more to lose?

At the Checkout Counter

When you are deathly ill
the kiddos come to say
"you can lick this"
"hang in there, you must stay"
"fight this old man, please fight it"
while sucrose drips in collapsed veins
morphine finds its way into a your right
hand offering mercy and brings reverie

in the haze you wonder for what to battle on
that gut pain that rises with you each day for
the last thirty years
hanging round until each tooth is yanked
medieval style, pain and screams aside

a man who contributed nothing much
only did less harm than most
who once stood tall and spoke clearly
with some measured eloquence
mumbles more than speaks
grunts as brawny orderlies,hum Otis Redding tunes
as they shove a tube up your ass

waiting for the enema bag to empty into
a tortuous colon, about out of peristalsis

live more to sit in that large worn chair
by the window,shoved open to smell the spring
fragrances
see sun come over haze
moon rise cast light upon a bay
as Lang Lang plays Debussy's
Claire de Lune

Can't remember my sons names
Alive and gone
Daughter's smiling face makes me
Cry
Stick around to swipe the ole' EBT
For chips and root beer
Circle the 460 foot room
Reach for the S and W loaded
With five hollow points, with no
bravado to squeeze one off

keep breathing in and out
to write more of what no one reads
say what no one wants to hear
pray to some ancient God, maybe still
there after 5,000 years?

I'm in the check out line
Waiting for Lang Lang's final note
Check me out, Judy
Time to go
And
keep the change

Stubborn Nation

This land of the free moves towards
its promise slowly
forcing change to come only after
voices rise
streets fill with marchers
riots burn and men suffer
push and shove across the
landscape of a short history
of a Republic so set in
its ways

a national character that has
fought off accepting Catholics,
Irish, Poles, Slavs, Greeks, Armenians
and every type of Jew
while taking in Africans in slave ships
just to count a few

500,000 died to end a tarnished past
But it took that to begin the march to
A nation truly dedicated to the "proposition
that all men are created equal"
and stiff necked resistance remained

for another hundred years
as lynching overcame right and reason
finally a country looked at itself and cried
as great men died

stubborn men held the franchise
until women forced it upon a nation
that could not say it was democracy
without their right to vote
took 132 years
and still no ERA

slave free
took a Civil War
women vote
took a 130 years
civil rights
marches, riots, assassinations
and the voices of change
with a righteous view, relentless
until the nation turned towards
what was next and inexorable on the way to a more perfect union

SpeedBalling at Chateau Marmont

She could fill a syringe
deftly
with cocaine and heroin
find a pulsing vein and
inject nirvana into
some big names brain

sultry brunette
full lips
alluring wide eyes
with a look that said
I'm a good time gal who will take you
places
you have never been
and rocket you there again and
again

Cathy Smith fueled the rockers
sang with some
supplied others
screwed with Lightfoot
and speedballed Belushi

at room #3 at the Chateau
on an otherwise ordinary March
night

artists get forgiven
being drunks, addicts or both
the work insulates, defines their
existence, what they do to stay
alive forgotten over time
and who put the needle in his
arm that night dies now only for that

Bobby D came by with his buddy
To say hello before they went off to
See Robin's improv show
Smith mixing the brew
Surrounded by piles of underwear,
Empty wine bottles, and pizza cartons
a distasteful milieu

Sundown thought nothing of it
really
It was what they all did do in 1982
Shoot up
Hang out at Dan Tana's
Lay out at the Roxy, hit up the Comedy Club
on Sunset, nightcaps wine and heroin
And drift away to that one safe
Place where no one or anything could
Get to them anymore

Somehow she made it to 73
The band life far away
Gave up 15 months of freedom
For her injection that day
deported to Canada, where she would stay
a woman of some attraction, to artists with
something to say, remembered for what they
wrote, and did, while she just fades away.

What Side of the Bed Did You Sleep On

Memory might be neutral
With no point of view, so
You could conjure whatever
It is that happened to you

Sparks of success and happiness
Perhaps, a smile or two
The first kiss, was it sweet or sour
a submersion into a woman who liked you
or so it seemed, until the tale of woes overtook
everything else, drowning your desires

milestones, once monumental
but heaps of gravel by life's road
graduations, degrees in obtuse things,
the race to being a master of the universe
on reflection, such wasted time

marriages forged in pretended love
children birthed, an expected legacy
of their creation, unable to bring to consciousness
a single time, where the light you shined
along their paths was bright enough to show

the way

faces come forward in the insomnia nights
mostly dead men now, recalling what expired them
than what made them whole or revealed their souls
realizing how few there were that offered you much or you
back to them

vividly recalling when you are still
the humiliations, errors in judgment, cowardly
repulsion from striking out boldly, so afraid of
shame, frightened by having nothing again,
the pain of counting quarters to do laundry,
sleeping in the car, the awful pretense that you
were very much alright, when you could not sleep
a single night for a full year
memories of comfort and safety do return
unwanted, and with no volition, when you are too
weary to fight your prohibitions
you recall her head on your shoulder, but which one
you wonder, did she sleep here or on the other side
and it comes to you, and you slide over, pretending she is there……

One Legged Wake Up Call

Easy to get strangled by petty misery
It constricts your blood flow in a carotid choke
Hold
It won't kill you, just put you to sleep after you
Gasp for air to stay alive

Whining, complaining nonsense
Mundane concerns of laundry, muscle
Pain somewhere, ever changing from back to neck
To groin

Unfulfilled promise, botched couplings,
Distant fathering, self –imposed silences
Avoidance over confrontation, living a small life
Not writ large

All emerge and converge as you step
Out under the deep grey marine layer
Wanting sun, finding neither it, nor sinking
Moon, to run it all back, back, into your
Medulla oblongata, to gain clarity
Or just delay
And you groan, and spit as you

Uncoil
Depressed hoping for enough elation to
Go one more step

And then she comes by
Tall and clean, bare midriff
Perfect face and ponytail
Running at a 7 mile pace
With one leg well and the other
A prosthesis, a carbon fiber miracle
That gives her bounce and speed

And you wonder what grave malady, accident
Contortion or misdirection took the right leg
Away
And left her this way

To run free of petty things
Grateful for one thing
That she could run free and flash smiles
Nod at tortured old men
And disappear into a fog

Cleansed me of the crap
Cleared a cluttered mind
Brought prayer to my lips
And left the miseries behind

What Do the Damn Critics Know

Anyway
On imaginary fences they dwell
Gargoyle heads and faces out of
Academic hell
Drooling at creations
Sharpening talons in their time
Ripping off flesh, diving for your
liver, as if you were Prometheus
chained to a rock, as eagles came and took
your organs, only to return your
agony another day

never good enough for any of them
so beaten by what they left behind
back in the Pale, under the Cossacks
boot
where they could never have their say
even as they were raped, and screwed from
behind, not allowed to curse or whimper
lest they be betrayed

that torch of Liberty burns bright
a fire of commentary and critique

endless babble, often wrong, but
always holding me back
their horizons close and unspectacular
do only what feeds them, houses, and provides
all else is frivolity and a genuine waste of your time

in time their rants became just more noise
they got old, shriveled, and died away
still their voices stayed
and I thought small, risked not enough
and could hear their whine, inside of me
on sleepless nights

never listen to the critics
they call to keep you contained
afraid that if you soar
they will be forgotten, not forgiven
for tarnishing what you could be
by listening to them

Moonglow

High in a cloudless sky
Moon stares full at me
Awakening for moment to
Piss into a nearby Big Gulp cup
Having drifted off empty into
Emptiness
Hollow unable to reach a soul
Inside

Conversation directed by toil
over
Silent Friday night
Projecting the soundless insanity of a long weekend
Idle
Blasting hip hop and wrap with high volume
Bass turned up, unbalanced
Echo up through the sound room of my life
The streets
And force noise canceling headsets
For solace

Broken and worn from inside out
At 4am walking towards a bay

To follow the moon as its glow moves
Across it, 288,000 thousand miles away
Sit in cold sand, hum Nessun Dorma, a few
Times
Let the light roam through me
Pretending it will renew
Rejuvenate, find whatever spirit resides
Within, and bathe it in its
Glow
Easy enough to find, as I am less
Bone and sinew than glass
The light goes through me
Casting not a shadow
Entering and exiting untouched
By anything

Just Another Day at El Pollo Loco

Just wanted a chicken bowl
And a diet Coke
Three average Washington D.C. gals
Who worked for some folks on Capital Hill
Average afternoon, mixed race patrons
Chatting away on a late summer day

Young terrorists arrive wanting to
Terrorize, tenderize, vilify and intellectually
Force rape the people inside
"raise your hands for Briona
Wipe out police brutality"
It seems to rhyme and they put their noses
To their faces and scream it louder
A few raise their hands afraid
But these girls
Refuse, and will not be forced to Seig Heil
If the tuffs knew what that might be
Lunatics, of the mob, with its own
Ideology, of fear and abuse

The girls are shaken but stand their ground
Their courage emerges as they stand their ground

No one goes after the violent bastard shrews
Who can only tell you Black Lives Matter
Which they think will silence you

You cannot disagree or you will be
Kicked in the head until you lose an eye
Shot dead on a street, and laugh as you run
Away
Have your store looted and they will say
"hey, its reparations old man, for the sins
Back in the day.. fuck you in the ass with
This stick anyway"

Righteous, true believers in nothing
By to destroy, easier it is than to create
Which requires skills, intellect, and desire
None of it here, in the El Pollo Loco
They leave after spitting on them,
And walking off with their chicken
Paying for nothing, stealing our freedom to just be
Left alone

Nietzsche on the Boardwalk

You can find deep thoughts anywhere
In most unusual, unexpected places
Even when its 98, along the boardwalk
Just south of LA on Labor day
In the hands of a homeless dude
With a prophets beard, long slacks and
No shoes
Holding a sign, scribbled with a marker found
discarded and buried under a Jersey Mike
wrapper

'God is Dead'

"Jesus is gone away"

I yell "Nietzsche … Nietzsche"

And he seemed bemused, maybe never heard
of the author of the phrase

it was science, the enlightenment that killed him
the philosopher did say, out of the mouth of an
invented madman in his own way

for once God is dead everything that requires
faith also dies
no more absolute values
no universal moral law
and what it leaves behind the
homeless along the wall knows
too well
nothingness, the expansive value of
nihilism
where might, and wealth, and elites
rule it all

perhaps this sign holder is not lost
at all, but a man wandering with a lantern
shinning light on us all
where are values now, as thugs rob
and beat, anyone dares say leave me
alone today

whose to say he was and is away
or gone forever, not just for the fellow
on the concrete wall, but to us all

Letting Go

It is rare to find or come across
A man who lives free and unbound
By the restraints of the everyday
Stumbling on along a life path whether
Chosen, imposed, designed, even
Mapped by another's hand

With his destiny tucked under his arm
Running tentatively, not without abandon
Gaining yards, workmanlike
His brain knocked enough against the skull
To bring on early onset cranial traumatic
Encephalitis

Is there a gene that clicks on
Locks us up, a living sphincter
Informing every action, a constant
Tension from gut to grip to jaw
Clenched?

It ensues without command
No one declares
Be quiet, circumspect

Watch out, there is hell to pay
Silence is rewarded, not outbursts of clarity
Do not ever say. You are fed up, weary
Uncertain, or fallen out of
Love, attention, devotion, commitment
And are just damn bored or even
Betrayed

Momentarily, it seems, as though I
Have arrived there in a dream
I'm running on a flat blacktop in the Mojave
And a voice emerges consciously, clear
As my mother's screams
"let go" "let go"
Of what need not be asked
There is a knowing of what I must
Not pass
Just take a breath, and relax
Let whatever I am gripping so hard
Go, let blood flow and crap it all out
By a mountain pass

Attached to everything, as if my attention
Mattered in the direction of it anyway
It all might advance as well without my
Holding on tightly
Sending me more quickly to a fate
Destined or not
Still better to just untie the Gordian

knot and banish tentative action
finally, and live without constant
calculation of outcomes and design

might life seem free and of my
volition just one time.

The Jew in The Middle
Circa 5780

First Jew arrived in 3761 BCE
When Jehovah made it so
When 6000 years go by the
Messiah, will arrive
In 2239 of our time
So we have a way to from
The New Year of 5780
219 years to go for salvation to
Come and all miracles can show

Gotta wonder is any Jews will be around
To pray on that fateful day
Only 15 million out of 7.5 billion
Barely a % point and
Yet,
Hard to ponder how they last
Blamed still for most rotten occasions
5780 years of wanting to just be free enough
To be, without the knife being at their
Throats, historically

The litany of woes is known, if avoided
By the tormentors that arise with every millennium
With the same worn narrative

God throws us out of Eden
Abraham impregnates Hagar
Ishmael and his mother are expelled
Issac lives, Jacobs begats the Twelve Tribes
Slavery to Exodus
David and Solomon bring on a 'gilted age'
Until Temple One is destroyed
Babylon comes, Cyrus relents
Jews rebuild until Rome arrives
Jesus enters and then is crucified
Rome and Titus destroys Temple 2 and everything inside
Tribes flee into the diaspora
Inquisition, banishment, torture, ghetto life,
Forced in the Pale by the Tzars
Plagues come and go
Jews massacred for poisoning the wells
Pope's roundup the Talmuds in France and burn them
With much glee
The holocaust comes and goes, and deniers
Proliferate across countries to hold on to
The Protocols of the Elders of Zion, after
All of the above believe that Jews are running
Everything

So at 5780 is this a good time to be a Jew
50/50 if they marry a Jew
Fewer are raised that way
The left wingers are alarmed, especially the blacks
That the Jew is behind redlining, systemic racism
and not flattening the COVID curves
The right has new conspiracy theories that can still
shout out "white nigger" to a congregation of caring souls
or claim through Q Anon that Jews are behind the riots
in the streets, secretly hoping for a race war

men with vacant eyes and distant stares
still bring Ar-15's to bloody synagogues
shoot fingers off Rabbi's, murder the sisterhood
even religious zealots who praise Allah
rip men to shreds for daring to create a cartoon
of the Prophet
and the world carries signs J suis Charlie!

Not a year of peace, not one
from Eden and 3761
what prophet of today would ever
dare say
we'll all be around when 6000
comes to stay

God willing!

I See Her Face

Everywhere
Not every day does it
Come into play
I am not obsessed, I promise
Yet, out of nowhere, my mind is caught
Strangely
Towards a face I came to love and do
still, sharing or not the excitement of life
blended with loss and unspeakable
tragedy

A woman with rainbow colored hair
Thick and mid back long
In a miraculous turquoise thong
I run around her, startled to find
The face I cannot see, next to me
Hazel eyes wide, set near enough
To an aquiline nose

Then there is Dr. Cynthia a forensic
Expert of some acclaim, opining away
on some criminal insight, and I am transported

back in time, her hair and face
and long hands sublime measures
of a woman once in her prime

on days like this the Gestalt shifts
I see her features in unlikely places
My mind a projector onto woman's
faces, even Streisand, in Two Faces in a Mirror
becomes her in the last reel, elegant, sexy,
and alive, not plain, and only smart as a bookish
Brooklyn Jew

Pretense dissolves
That I am over her the pain of
a walk away not in the past
this day

That face rests deep inside
Present when it comes to the fore
A cohort of feelings you cannot
Ignore,
To distractions I amend, the afternoon
Playing Sammy in Berlin singing a favorite
Tune
"what kind of man is this
An empty shell
Lonely cell in which
An empty heart must dwell"

Unsatisfied still turning
To the baritone of Dimitri Horoskovsky
Sending a message of warning to his
Sister, Margarita and hum
through the tears
head towards an empty beach
where no music plays

I know, I know
The face is no longer there on the pillow
Nearby, yet,
Indelible
A tattoo on my heart
With a firm grip on my tortured soul

The sun exits a sky tinted by wildfires
Saturates the bay, orange, and bathes me in its light
Only expands my despair, she is not by my side
So I cannot see the beauty of it all, in her eyes.

How Men Die

Some die angry
Over everything gone wrong
Never heard of one dying humming a song
Resigned to moving on and ending
The pain, actual, they have been through
As the doctor gods tried to save you

Most without a tear
None afraid to go
Most knowing the darkness is coming
Better than those who are taken by
The forces
Suddenly
With no goodbyes, machinations
Just faded

Dad died in his own bed in that rowhouse
Shrunken down to 90 pounds
Could have taken a bullet from a Jap in Burma
Been knifed in Mandalay
Run over by a Frank's truck in South Philly
But he died in my mother's arms in the very
Bed they shared for 50 years

Old Joe died there as well
In my sister's room vacant now
That housed him near the end near 100
15 feet by five, coffin like anyway
Just plain old age got him,
could have been in the alley by the pool hall
after taking two guys cash, once hustled by pops and
Moscone, Senior, not
after all those
Depression days, six kids, and a wife gone the last
Four decades

Men die in all the ways you can depart

Jerry rolls over one night before his show on
MSNBC, pancreatic cancer

Ron, goes early from lung cancer, after a life of
Smoking a few packs a day

Jim says goodbye, leaving behind a warehouse or two
of booze, piles of cocaine, tar and nicotine, and a chorus line
of babes, longer than a football field

None of them sees 65

Jimmy Bouton had a great arm, and a raucous laugh
Forgot who he was in the end, strangled by amyloid
plaques

Mutty got home from the Ardennes, untouched, but skinny as hell
Lived a while, until a tumor evolved in his brain, they blew
His head up pumpkin size, didn't help at all
That wife who looked like Jane Russell
Never opened the casket, to shield him from her mother's
View

Mikey was so confused after a life of struggling
With his impulses and his crappy brain chemistry
Drove his truck to a local Jersey river and
Put his hunting rifle to his head
And said goodnight on Xmas eve
Before 30

Then the forces came for Gabe
One a trip back to Penn State
His buddy lost control on a patch of
What they call "black ice"
Car smacked a tree, broke the young man's neck
Everyone lived but him
Checked out at 19

Men die in different ways
Rarely leave an epitaph
No notes to offer solace to those left
Behind
No drum rolls and trumpet calls
No 24 notes of taps
Just here and then departed
Mostly without ceremony

Leaving sadness as legacy
Hoping to reverse Shakespeare
The good they leave behind lives after them
And the evil that men do is buried
And apart of their souls become part of us.

The NFL Played Again

At what was Hollywood Park
The NFL played again today
to no one in the stands
everyone afraid of this damn
novel virus that's taken over the land

In the USA
1,000 died of it today
Adding up to 200,000 they say
Mostly old folks or anyone fat, with bad hearts
And even diabetes, which is almost one out of two
Pre existing conditions, taking down a few

In Iran
Navid Afkari, a wrestler is hung at dawn
For the crime of speaking up to the mullah
goons, his two brothers still tortured
and all chained up

In D.C.
Israel signs a peace deal
With the UAE and Bahrain

Justin Kustner get the blame
No one wants to praise a pact made
on Trumps watch

In LA
a short black guy walks up to
two cops in a black and white
fires and runs away
BLM assassin caught on tape
Nowhere to be found, no one speaks up
As the cop mother bleeds from a shot up jaw
And her partner, 24, bleeds from his arm

Bad enough, you might surmise

Then a surprise comes outside
The ER, where the cops fight to live
And the mother hopes to see her kids
The BLM banshees come and scream
"I hope you die"
"I hope you Pigs die"
Until they are escorted away
Another venomous display of
What has become of this world
On this September day.

Drinking Ants at 5:45

Dawn breaks late as
long summer days are abbreviated by
the solstice of fall
no sun in my eyes at the usual AM
place to urge me awake
in darkness then

to toilet bowl, stumbling over
shoes and clothes, laundry still
waiting to be done
filling that orange mug
with a Jaguar logo offered up
by a hopeful salesman way back in the day
when I was a master of the universe

gargle it
turn on a light
start the obligatory brushing routine
observe the aged face, the wrinkled brow,
the Cyrano nose, enlarged ear lopes,
thinning lips, untouched by others for
many years, and the teeth of a dying man

gnarly now, once collectively admired
in what once were easy smiles
except additionally

a colony of wayward ants
crawling across my bicuspids
creeping through the spaces as though
I was already Yorricks' skull pulled in
untimely fashion from my given
hole

everywhere they were
from cup to brush
massed and crawling past
exploding my attention just\towards
them, and coughing them up
as if in mid nightmare
knowing that I as well awake

Drown the bastards as if they had no place
Being there, even though they had as much
Natural reason, if not more than me
Until the sunlight came orange over my
Shoulder, and returned me for a moment to
Morning bliss
No danger here
Not more than a few hundred tiny
Ants could bring

Reminding me that I could be unraveled
By not so much or placid or serene
And it was only all up to me
To be either.

Gross Hematuria

And now a poem about
Piss
That should never be a problem
A natural act for mammals of all
Sorts
Lifted dog legs abound around
Hydrants to Rudy's Doberman leaking
On your front tire outside the bar

Goats, cows and race horses let it
go without hesitation
elephants flood the sawdust at the circus
and I swear I saw a Rhino smile in mid
urination

in younger years a grand relief, a
relaxation, beer filled bladders,
the piss through wood after a
night of the in and out
full, clear, flow from bladder to bowl
or anywhere when it was time
as the years go the prostate grows

slower for some but for all
an internal clock marking your going
buddy, not now, but in its own time
blood after a long run, a rugby game,
or passing one damn painful kidney stone

you can see it now, and it scares you
to hell,
"why is there blood in my urine, Doc"
"its gross hematuria"
"yeah, so how bad is it"
"can't tell, do this until it goes away"

Exits for you
But not for Vegas Dan, a formidable man
Eggs and sausage for breakfast, and red meat for lunch
Can drink all day, fuck all night, and still be all in
At the poker table
Now he's rolling craps

Gross hematuria
His lumbar discs shot
His kidneys spitting out calcium studded stones
Sense of humor only thing left
Intact,
No urinal ever past or fountain not
Water taken

Just a regular piss is not much to ask
An ancient function from our primal past
Once a rapids of urine, now a damned stream
No more time to wonder what any of it means
Just one week, one week, of just pissing clean
Like when he was a bull all of sixteen.

No Time To Dream

Hours get crowded
What you have to do and must
Gobbles the minutes
Grazing some more, moving with
Purpose an hour or so
Doing what you need to do to
Realize what's next only a few tocks
Of all the ticks

You know you cannot move from
Where you are to where you want
To be
Unless you change the patterns
Here
And you don't stymied by convention
Lack of contention and the pure false
Security of doing what you always have
Again and again

Reverie comes, quickly fades
Surfing Waikiki, mounting the Matterhorn,
Screwing gals in some foreign red zone,
Making a damn difference for someone

Besides you, and even changing your direction
Less than three minutes an hour, for most
working men

must everything implode, explode, pummeled
into ash, for our consciousness to shift away
from our tightly held and cherished tarnished
past?

Stubborn, rutted lives
Happy, joy, and even fulfilment
Excluded or forced into an hour or so
On a computer display
Allowing time off, by some unseen
Overseer, time earned to be away
To what?

A life lived in hours
Consumed by the must and matters
Not enough for what I might be or do
Enjoy, love, or just do
An insanity of sameness, deluded that it
Will all change, miraculously
which it never does
still you pretend in
Reflection it
was a worthwhile day, afraid to face
your regrets, for dreams left for
another man, more inclined to say
"I can't live like this anymore"

Swimming to Galilee

Standing on the shore where Christ
appeared
a lake called a sea filled then
with fisherman now
serene,
where grand moments occurred captured
in scripture

Jesus off recruiting here
Place of teaching, activity, not
Reflection
Simon and brother Andrew collected
Their nets and found their way to him
Then
John and James
one Jew about to be Christ
came with a God directed purpose

not I this day
the Jordan still flows into Galilee
as it did in his day
I throw a rock and pray as the
Ripples undulate towards me

It is dawn and I walk into the ancient
Sea
Take 500 strokes out
Turn and contemplate my own absurdity
Alone on this Father's day

Then between pulls through the
dark green waters
a roar comes over me, enormous sucking
sound, I go under instinctively
coming up for a breath as it passes

two fighter jets 20 feet above me
out for a morning mission
breaking the calm, serenity
replacing the soft focus
shattering my reverie
returning to what is, not was or
might be

Not seeking baptism
Just a quiet morning swim
solace, touching what
came before, yearning for
epiphany
in my reflection by
the Sea of Galilee

Pipe Dreams

O'Neill had them put them
Into plays, until the booze got him
And ate his brain away
From a hotel room in Boston
Sheraton 104, he gave his characters flaws
That they only could survive
With pipe dreams in their eyes

Do men have them at all
Anymore
That allows them to go on, holding
A thought inside their mind, reaching for
A string of better days
A life lived far, far away from where they
Are today

Muse, goal, item on a
Bucket list kept secretly inside a bedroom's
Drawer,
Or just what we used to call a lie
Knowing we cannot do it, reach it,
Plan or obtain it at all,
But

Without it we are done
Unable to forgive ourselves without
Even a honest effort to achieve it
And step away free, if worn
From the current day to day that has certainly
Taken our dreams away

Pipe dreams are about
Somedays, and then, I wills
I will do, and you'll see
All devoid, by their nature of current
Reality
But without them where would men
Be
We all need our illusions to buffer us from
Despair
Safe havens of deception,yet, a place to go
When the slap of any moment returns us to
The now, and knock us to the ground
Hold onto that pipe dream
Do not let it fade it away
Imagine more to help you maneuver
Through more days
There must always be a carrot on
Some proverbial stick
Just out of touch something, just beyond your grasp
Put it on a paper scrap and carry it with you
To contemplate on lost days
And sit with it, for a time, calculate how to make it true
And don't let anyone take it

It's your pipe dream, and it belongs to you
Keep them always or
That Iceman will Cometh to your wife too
Catch them screwing each other and you
And you'll blow them both away
Before your pipe dreams can come true…..

The Glory that was Rome

The Temple was long gone
rubble and dust remained
Titus took the treasures
Murdered Jews along the way

Some revolted, all died away
Then Bar Kokhba came, some thought
He was the Messiah once named
Wrong they were, of course
Hadrian and his lackey Turnus
Rufus felt no remorse
The Jews were colossal irritants
No more than that to be
Eradicated under a Roman sandal

So then an ancient court decreed
Wherever Jews might be
The elders could not teach
The five books of Moses and pass on
The word to the flock
And if they dared defy the edict
They would die
Each rabbi, they could find

Rabbis 'of the time did not
Hide, or cower, taught the word
As though the Romans 'had no fervor
To crush a faith that was a bur and burden
of stiff necked Hebrews who fought back
from time to time

They took the Kohen Gadol, Ishmael
Who wanted to be the first to die,
But Rabbi Shimon asked for the same fate
They drew lots, and Shimon won and was
Beheaded
Ishmael raised his head in his hand and
Claimed that the tongue that uttered prayers
"now licks the dust"
They then flayed his face

The storied Rabbi Akiba recited the most holy prayer
The Shema its called that simply says
"here o Israel, the Lord our God, the Lord is one"
And he continued as the Roman executioner ripped off his
skin with iron combs
The Lord is One- the final words, as the Roman slave
Gathered the skin and severed heads

Judah ordained five rabbi's in the back hills
They found him
And three hundred lances shredded his body
Even as
Rabbi Hanina ben Tradyon taught in a public square

Wrapped the book of Torah around him and covered his heart
With wet wool, so he would suffer more
And died with soft prayers on his lips
And the town people wept

No mercy from Romans who had their own
Gods and celestial design. They feared less the
Uprising of these "children of God" than they did
The wrath of their overseers
Eventually even they died 500 years later
To the thugs of their time, who couldn't find a
Jew to kill, so they began to thrive
Until darkness came to them
Again and again
Knowing
There will always be Romans

Loosen the Grip on the Rudder

Hand is cramped from holding
The rudder tightly
Delusional in believing the course
I'm charting is of my making
A vessel of life directed towards
Some terrestrial place worthy of
Attention and devoted undertaking

Am I headed to that someplace, still
contemplated but largely unknown
is that not Bali Hi, or but a mirage shielding
the destination of oblivion

at dawn the lifeboat is beached at the bay
I run on the ocean side where the moon full
Lays down a glow over the waves
Two surfers run and do not stop towards it
a woman wrapped in clothes as though she is
in Nome Alaska, settles to meditate her face
reflecting orange light

then ambling towards a sky brightening
a sun rises as I sit pissing in the sand on

Hugo's catamaran
Take a breath
Watch it rise,full, unblocked by cloudy
mists and sigh
wanting to be frozen there, a few nanoseconds
of rotation delayed
let someone else worry how the world
will get by

Trump has the COVID
Melanie has it too
Airlines lay off 56,000
Disney drops 38 thousand
Danny's band is wearing Wal Mart vests
To pay 25 % of their rent
Big Joe is sleeping in his car, outside Louis' bar

Not much about it, I can resolve
Running back to that rudder reapplying the
Grip
A long legged, full lipped gal pulls behind me,
Her footsteps irritate, I resolve to not let her or anyone
Pass me on the last miles back
I run until I can't hear her breathing
One act of pure volition that for that
moment I can actually have a say
Unlike anything else that happens
Today.

Wonder What It Is Like Struggling with Fame

Zeppo came by to just say Hi
to John's cottage just north of Monterey
where he wrote novella's, books, and even
plays
unknown for most of words exploding from brain
to page until he hit on George and Lennie
that made its way to Broadway
Steinbeck never even returned a reply
To a Marx brother with an accolade

Chaplin came around in a limo that
Even the reclusive soul could not dispatch
Even as the pain of being known brought
The author to near collapse
Chain smoking his way to a story roaming
Inside him gnawing its way out
Until it was exposed

He heard the hymn until the title appeared
"he is trampling out the vintage where the
grapes of wrath are stored"
wrath indeed, of stories too real to

for any common man, of dislocation,
hardship, disease, neglect, abandonment
forsaken by forces big and small

capturing on a page again
the valor and spirit of characters created
by his wood burning stove, and lack of
adequate light, except that which came form
within, enough to win
the Pulitzer Prize, and a movie with Jimmy
Stewart too

Fame came and had its own demands
marriages ebbed and meandered
not like his writing which still flowed
even as few friends entered the stage and
left before ACT lll
depressing more a man adjusted to the created
life, between the hard covers, than the life
adjusted to the run on sentences of an icon's
day to day

what could be more sublime than a Pulitzer and Nobel
in your prime
to have your pages turned to celluloid
rub shoulders with the red carpet crowd
have your name on school teacher's lips
books vilified and acclaimed
creating a literary stir, encouraging folks
to read something elevating, of your contemplation

is it all too much to pay
for the solitude you really seek each day
where no one can touch you, as you journey
into a theme that settles you and forces the
mess of the world to go away

Faustian for those of us unknown
Who would trade a soul for our story
On the Great White Way
Jimmy Stewart in the lead for big John Ford
or just to say
Come on in Zeppo, how are you, Today?

Leopard Bikini Under a Harvest Moon

There are no harvests nearby
to require a moon to signal the arrival
of high wheat or any other crop
where agriculture still thrives and
thick handed men direct tractors from
cabs with the internet and you tube songs
inside

concrete fields of men stayed too late
at office enclaves
women wanting to be elsewhere
quickly to hug a neglected face
rub a dog's belly, forget the
daily yes and no's, and recede
eventually to silence by the 11 o'clock news

so another moon, now risen galactically large
not seeming 250,000 miles away
throws barely enough light to save a
short girl with daisy dukes cut past ass check
high, attracting every jogger, as the German
Shepard she is pulling just sits, and decides to howl

At the bright disk in the sky, and the old man with the
French bulldog laughs, as he stoops to put his animals
Crap into a pink plastic bag, commemorating breast cancer
Week, day, or month

I pull over
turn off everything
Take ten deep breaths and attempt to
Turn my consciousness back to detach and drift
Away from connected, angry, and lost

A thin, long gal rides on a very ancient
Cruiser straight at me, as I rest on the bumper
Contemplating nothing more than the moon
She stops, says, in Carol Channing voice
"hey, good looking"
Reveals her lanky frame in a two piece
Leopard skin bikini, with barely a bottom
And a top of a girl of 16

Nothing more than just a high and howdy
To be sure, and a smile to match the
Moon's light, Cheshire like on this

October night

She shows me her skinny ass
Shakes it for good measure
Gets on the bike and
Rides off towards the marine layer
About to obliterate everything

Used to enjoy sunsets and moon glow
More about sunrise now
Fewer people and the pretention that
It brings another shot at having a
Day worth something, and no
Crying in your beer

You were Happy When

Neck is so stiff it can be hard
to see an on coming semi only hear it
need a rear view mirror to see the debris
of the life you've lived and left behind
and attempt a glimpse along that rutted
path of anything, person, or time where
you were, what the guru's call

happy

was it ever on your agenda
as you moved through life's markers?
so intent on achieving, recognition
in an unending quest for relevancy
just to establish to yourself that you were
worthy, of praise, esteem, the earned
life of purpose, or so you believed

walking through snow drifts
to catch a train to NYC to spend a week
alone after work, in a 100 square foot
Tudor City flat, with a murphy bed that opened
into the bathroom, and you could scramble eggs

on a stove, while still in bed
living in the car, parked on a quiet street
changing clothes at the park restroom after
rousting the regulars, a new cake of Safeguard
soap as a peace offering

can you catch happiness, even for a moment
or so, before you drive your standard four door
into a concrete wall, stop and jump off the Coronado
or Golden Gate at high tide
is it just so that a man's life is inoculated from it
unable to catch any recurring dream
where you walk around with a smile
sustained, and let the usual grimace go
away
for a moment

flashes of it there and then
first kisses, loves, rush of marriage vows, affairs, births
promotions, cash, finish lines of all sorts, beating down
bastards in and out of court, a hot shower, a quiet bed,
an afternoon nap, with nothing in your head, a single day
where everyone you know or care about is just
ok
so it's there, flashes of brightness in between the
grey life

and what of it ahead
as your nose grows, ear lobes sag
teeth yellow and hurt at night

age enters every vein, shrinkage
comes to once muscled limbs
and you are starting to just fade
away, every picture taken shows a smaller
man

better find some more of it
might sustain the hit of a life
lived hard, and full, with more than its
share of upsets, and losses
a touch on a man's shoulder encouraging
enough to get you out of bed and on your way
before that semi takes you

He Just Wanted to Get Laid

Jakarta, Indonesia
10 September 2020

Monty could not know when
He swiped left to hook up
With a big bosom, long leg
chick, all full lips, blazing white teeth
and large hands
that he would end his in and out
excursion, in eleven pieces inside a
hefty garbage bag

he was only 32 dying
to screw, get blown and
lose it for an hour or two
inside this brunette who said all
she wanted was IT, nothing more

mounted her face to face
she pumped him hard kept him in
his place, moaned a bit, rolled her

eyes back until all he could see was
the white of her eyes
and then no more

Monty has his skull cracked by a
brick in her boyfriends hand
takes a few more bludgeons but
still murmurs, signifying he is still alive,
boyfriend stabs him 24 times until
the blood, and gurgles, and sucking
sounds told boyfriend he was gone

she took a shower, ate a few crackers
sipped a beer
visited the local hardware store
debated, argued and decided on a
machete and a saw
laid out some black plastic bags
and hacked Monty into 11 pieces
not counting his head
that was in a doggy bag

no motive of complexity
cash for stuff is all
oddity,perhaps, in what they bought
nothing more
motorcycle, some gold, jewelry for her,
new panties, a black helmet, and
rented an apartment for them to stay

and practice the bliss that comes from
cashing in on a guy who just wanted
to get laid, in Jakarta, on a September
afternoon.

You Need to Get Out and Date

A phrase from another time
before the www age, when women
in search and men in search of different
outcomes pretend they are after the same
thing
men lie, women exaggerate, but say what
they desire, more than dinner and a roll
in a bed that is

had the lunch dance
pranced around a dinner table
sipped a bad Bordeaux
thought a root canal more pleasant
just one probe assisted by drugs
to alleviate the pain

who can listen for an hour and a half
to the biographical path of these tortured
women, where they came from, college path or not,
the wonder of their progeny, the evil of the ex
even though the current discovery of their
purpose is funded by the hapless SOB
flirting gets me nowhere

across the table I can see I am more
like the father they all loved
who gets up at night to pee

never minded being alone, anyway
if I need an aspirin I take it
stay up until 3 am, reading Tropic of Cancer
wash the car at 4
carry a .38 to the ATM
nap when I can, and ask for nothing in return
with no one asking, why

a solitary guy, who can go a day
with uttering sound or word, and realize
that saving up a grand for a colossal piece of ass
makes no sense, the money better used
for pants, shoes, a sweater, underwear and socks
and getting the carpet cleaned, and buying bread and
a new toaster
so when one calls and says "I'd like to see you again"
"I'm too busy this week Lorraine,
Call you, another time."
Yeah, Right!

The Belt in the Box

The world is often out of place
Helter Skelter when you are 13
You feel something about to happen
or emerge and you wait for it
endlessly
everyone has anecdotes, parables
suggestions and reflections on what you
should explore, desire, and even adore
while you're just trying to find the key to
your own damn door to knock on

visiting my uncle Nate behind this guy
Moe's Kosher Butcher store sat Moe
With a box behind him, he looked about
22
And the box had a belt inside it
About a 34 -36 I suppose
But it had pronounced notches as it went
From 34- 25 or so

Moe relaxed, sat back, with an apron of
Blood, and rested his thick hands in his lap
"that's my Auschwitz belt"

I wore it there, you know Auschwitz, right"
I nodded
"three years, and almost every few weeks I cut another
Hole, until there was nothing left, then the Russians came"

When I got old enough to have a real job
I bought a belt, vowed to keep it until the work
Stopped, had it on the day I visited Moe's shop
after the service and the prayers, Moe got to 80
and the belt was always there a reminder
of that evil past

They gave it to me, and I put it in a drawer
Until I took it out one Saturday and prayed
That mine would always be the same, wear out
One notch, over a lifetime of paying bills, taking care
Of everyone along the way, so I wear mine, even as it frays
So I won't forget Moe, and those Auschwitz days

Where Did All The Strippers Go

Silent now on stages
Where women gyrated on these
Polished poles
Where platform shoes still stomped
And G strings went undone
Nipples covered at places timid in
their time
floors scuffed by gals crawling on all fours
to sailor boys, fork lift operators, UPS guys
and who know from where guys playing
mogul for a night with a fist of dollars
and twenties in each hand

Down at Cheetah's and Pacers
Over at the Body Shop and Crazy P
Only the owners hanging around with
Pedro and Raul trying to keep the places
Clean

Charlene is at Walmart in a vest showing folks
To aisle 8
Doris is cleaning at night with her boyfriend
Eugene, downtown

Eve is cutting hair and doing nails in
Compton with her sister
Big Sue is still dancing for guys who can still
Party hardy at a secluded ARBNB

Roxanne and Lucy are in one studio with their
Three kids, helping them through school
Collecting any cash they can and pooling
Their EBT's

Who cares for them
These forgotten women of the small stage
That brought grown men, adolescent joy
Raised their wood on lonely nights and
Forlorn afternoons
Stood over them and jiggled their assets
For paltry pay
Who stands for them, considers them at all
As deserving as the rest, left out, looking
In to see if they can find a place to be
Until the lights go on again.

A Little Woman With a Green Wig

Screams at me after I say
No
I'm just waiting to pay for the
Usual evening crap meal after a
Week of work
Some microwave fake spaghetti
No meat chicken
Pretzels for desert
And a jumbo 99 cent ice tea

5' 3", no teeth
Dressed in green pajamas
Petal pushers pants from 1963
Very tan, leather like that only
Old cowboys and homeless can obtain
Out day and night on the plains or
or lost in concrete canyons with no exits

a skull emerging from thinned skin
and an enormous frightful wig
Phyllis Diller mane
Neon green
Standing next to me with a full

Super large coffee cup
Held up to my chin
"buy it for me mister"
and without a thought I say
"not now, no!"
I say in the unkindest way
supported by the Cambodian cashier
"get out, Doris, get out or I'll call a cop"

To which she screams at me
"I'm not on drugs, I'm not on drugs,
It's a fucking cup of coffee"
I pay, give her buck
"here now calm down, alright"
"fuck you"
The universal cry of distain, from all outsiders
Looking in

I sit in the car, and fume
Not at her but me
Where is that pledge to be kind
Fight the demons inside, she didn't need
mine, just a hot coffee to warm her insides
between hits of meth or crack
or who knows what
it just can't be that difficult to open
the kindness door
but it is on a Friday night
after the world seems insane
and you couldn't sleep, everything you ate

gave you cramps,
no one called to say hello, just to complain
or ask for cash
enough excuses, to get a celestial pass?

Am I so lost in the comfort of my own despair
to not be awake to see that life has but
bruised me, left scabs healed to scars
not obliterated my consciousness and
pulverized my spirit
lame excuses, the best of you
unrevealed as you
Could only say NO, to the
Poor 90 pound soul in the
Green wig.

Even the Soap Dish Must be Cleaned

What is obvious gets attention
What you expect to do gets done
Laundry is collected, quarters found
and hoarded, detergent rationed for the
months ahead

even the sheets get stripped on occasion
after months of studied neglect
vacuum cleaners borrowed across a year long
lease, to take the debris out of the 400 square
foot place

a rainy afternoon prompts it's the
day to get the refrigerator cleaned
throw out the old salad, partially used
water bottles, stale beer, cola long ago without its
fizz
and toss the frozen banana peels, stored in the
freezer to avert their decay

take a morning before the commute to
scrape the toilet bowl
polish the tub of the crud hard water brings

rip away a shower curtain, blacked over
once pure white, neglected

bow to the tiles
on hands and knees wash the floors
collect the dust and hair that has
collected there

convinced it is all done
even as the ants swarm from aged
pipes over the domain, crossing
in a pre dawn raid on that soap dish
of pewter that you've had for all the married years
and washing it now, involuntary memory ensues
bringing you to tears, the image in a mirror that
does not hide the emotions or the years
of all that you paid attention to and all the
things you did not.

The Religion of Woke

The screamers in the streets
The lost boys, who yearn to be men
Breaking windows, pissing in stores
Invaded by them and the opportunists
from the neighborhood, black men who know
better, whose mothers would cry if they saw them
walk away with liquor and television screens
as the tear gas replaces the night air
and gunpowder fumes fill flared nostrils

what passes for an intellectual sits
sipping latte with swirls, stirs with a cinnamon stick
contemplating a philosophy of Woke
hardly Kant, Sartre, Proudhon, Marx or James
Baldwin, just the narrative of pent up emotions,
of pay back and retribution

liberals said yes to debate, believed, reason could overcome
a room full of lies
argued for decades, but never shut off open argument
or that old favorite ideal, of is has to be what it is
empiricism is what you can observe and see

to be Woke, you need no investigation, rumination or
interpretation
the truth, you see, are already known
and the chosen will tell you what is true
and the hell with you, if you dare to disagree
we will loot, burn, and screw with you
endlessly, until you take a knee and offer
up a prayer to be left alone

it is an ideology without ideas
the mob is the tool
for a secular religion that worships
only what they say, from their condos
high above the avenues that their cohorts trash

get the Gulags ready
prepare the internment camps
find a place for the un Woke
people of thought and reason
or stand by for an uprising
that throws postmodernism to the curb
and washes its progeny into the sewer
where false Gods go

Goodbye Columbus

The dude thought he sailed to another place
Wound up on a tiny island
Enslaved who he could to gather and
transport goods to F and I
sailed, explored and exploited
a man of his time, barely exalted

ruled the places with a harsh hand
even for his century, was a stern
bastard to all, and F and I eventually
made him disinvited and history let him
be until here in America 1891, this
happened to Italians who came here for
other reasons, like a better life

New Orleans had a police chief shot
rounded up nine Sicilians
tried them all for murder, all were acquitted
left them in the local lock up with two others
languishing there

Mayor Joe Shakespeare stirred up a crowd who
Hated wopes and dagoes, thousands of them stormed
the jail, strangled, shot, and hung all eleven
most thought it just

Teddy wrote his sister
"I think it rather a good thing"

And the New York Times, a rag like all the others
"they are the descendants of bandits and assassins..
are a pest without mitigation"

The Sons of Italy of the day, got together to start resurrecting
Columbus, build statues to change the view, and underline that
Italians made America was it was too
The unloved, the pretentious, the evil boys of now
Throw chains around the image, and toss it into rivers
In otherwise quiet towns, not knowing or giving a damn
of why the statue stands
a symbol of hate and prejudice that murdered innocent
men, whose only crime was being from a far off place
no one could care to understand
The most sordid lynching in the USA was of Italians
All of it forgotten today…

And the Dawn Comes

Under a black sky, a soldier in fatigues, on his way
To a base somewhere, revs his Harley engine, and it
Sputters and whines, me awake
Not wanting dawn to arrive
Too many items on the list of what must be
Done
To justify even being here

All these affirmations, attestations,
proclamations, presenting a defense of
existence, for a man passed his prime
still in the rutted routine of the master of
the universe days

gargle, brush the teeth
swallow a glass of warm water
run the water hot, soften the stubble
shave, the exact same strokes since
you were 15, left handed
take a few breaths with no conscious thoughts
set your mind in a zen plane
check all the headlines in the usual places
from the lying New York Times to Hamilton's

Post, checking Reuters and the AP, to assure the
world was mostly in its place, unchanged from the
night before, when you collapsed during the late
news

then just as darkness begins to yield to some light
put on something white, so the trucks can see you
and the dame with the eyeliner and the cellphone
can't mistake you for homeless man as she floors her
BMW through the yellow light
get in the days roadwork, pretend you are Patterson
or Rocky, Balboa that is, on the way down Delaware
Avenue

Out its dark, back the dawn has come, without fanfare
With nothing more valiant to do than whittle away at the
lists of relevancy, to secure your pretension that you
still matter, somehow, and you suck it up

knowing other dawns meant more
for the men at Dunkirk, the 101st jumping behind the lines,
the shelling returning at Hue during Tet, the morning a leg is
lost, two buddies are taken by a sniper, or even the dawn
that comes with a sunset victory

if it is nothing more than, but, another return of light
from the black of night, signaling another day for an old
soul
that will be enough, as it always is, for men expecting just
another day and nothing more than that.

No Miracle on 34th Street

Seems he was always there
Come Xmas
Even before the Civil War
Rowland Macy imagined it
Away on whaling boats as a boy
at sea
the round, bearded gent with a
belly laugh, all in red and black boots
and gloves

an attraction every year
kids dragged by parents away from
the demands of the war, depressions,
more wars, periods of hope, polio fears,
mutual assured destruction, the red scare,
McCarthy, Watergate, assassinations,
JFK, MLK, RFK, riots, Rodney, Floyd,
Enough looting to scare you into joining the
NRA, and wonder how you pay off the mortgage,
the college debt, and keep the IRS away, all the while
hoping the bums in DC don't scam away your
Social Security that they took out of your wages
every other Friday, since you were 16

Santa was always there at the end
of the Thanksgiving Day parade, up the escalator
in the store on 34th, surrounded by elves, with green
faces, and red cheeks
lines long, with most children scared of the old fat
man, who did his best to calm them for a Q and A
a picture, and a candy cane

not there this year
after 160 years, not a war or
economic decay, just a virus called
Covid-19
A new Scrooge destroys Xmas cheer
Lethal to a few, frightening all the rest
Santa stays at the North Pole and takes
Your request virally to avoid spreading
The virus straight to you
Cookies and warm milk perhaps
More likely better libations for
a year of death and fear
one bourbon, one scotch, one beer

Petty Misery

Historians and all the other no it all
pundits push the premise in all
probability it is
the big things that move men towards
consequential change that
events are only triggers of some deeper
malaise
freedom, equality, repression, narcissistic
oppression, the rise of the individual, fed up
with divine right, confederation, the Pope
and all other high minded anti- social
manifestations

pick an ideology, they are all the same in their
view of revolution, of claims of Locke, Rousseau,
even, mean old Hobbes, Marx and Engels, of course
with the proletariat feed up with the exploitation of the
bourgeois, rebellion it would seem all about grander
things than

petty misery
which is what I see and hear when I listen
anywhere

"He parked the fuck right in front of me.. the bastard"
"All I wanted was to not pay the rent, for a few months, Christ"
"And the mother fucker put a nail under my tire, really.. really.. because I cursed his mother"

no job, packaged food, a piece of fruit
,usually a banana once in a while, never get
a call to just say high, always about cash, some
perceived indiscretion, ending with an admonition
that will spoil any worthwhile daydream

take away what makes you whole or
gives you some reason to rise for one more day
no work, no love, and then all that's left is to
rise above it and say
whatever the forces bring, I can stand against them
and go on
which in its declaration is a force in itself for
resilience and life affirming

they can't take my outlook, totally control
the mind, not yet anyway
when the freedom is gone and the petty misery
stays then, the uprising comes
so I can pretend
if all of us, rail against it, the
misery will fade and it will be worth it
to go for another day ....

On The Drive Back to the 475 Square

I'm ending a week of the standard
back and forth creeping away from sanity
clawing back towards it, afraid of losing myself
to stay in line, signed up and just paid for my
damn time
dwindling away each night, anyway hoping for
a sunrise
on this blue moon night, moon glows on the
brunettes face at the last red light, before my
highway commute, unfolds, stop less, so I can conjure
untrammeled scenarios
under the moon in Taurus

will the ex finally call and emancipate me
financially, and I can say, "he's one lucky guy
to be with you" what else could I say to finally end the
fiction that someday…she will say, come back

that mega million in my lucky place
in the back of my wallet, folded eight times
hiding the jackpot, will hit and I'll immediately
give a million each to the kids, and my sister in
Jersey, produce those film scripts in the suitcase

under my bed, start a new political party for common
folks like me, give away some of it to philanthropy,
buy a shack in the desert, a condo in Kona, and run
the tables in Vegas, fly to Frankfurt and Aruba to get
laid, and sleep a week in Moorea, in a hut over a
warm bay

turn off the freeway and get hit with
Friday night regrets, as always, pushing out the
endorphin rush of good thoughts, why did I hit
Cosmo and break my arm in places, miss Vietnam
And spend time in glory places; not run for Congress
back in the day, over play my hand and shoot off my mouth
when I took all the wrong stands, reverse a long line
of errors and bad calls, on the wrong path traveled
and visualize them all
Find an actual parking spot that will not require being
Doubled jointed to get in or out, the Doberman is not there
to growl as you pass, and the .38 is still in the glove compartment
untouched again
and the only thought left is to defrost the lean cuisine and turn on
Jeopardy, say a prayer of thanks, and collapse.

Speaking Freely while Being Strangled

Saying what's on your mind, lately
Speaking freely?
Afraid of being named something you are
Not
Do her girlfriends claim you exhibit
Toxic masculinity because you
Watch football on Sunday
Lift weights, still gaze at other women
In the mall, strut at times walking the hall,
Curse from time to time
Are silent and sublime, have a short
Attention span and actually own a
Shotgun, and a truck

After all you're just that
"common man" once saluted and
even revered, who could put a semi-truck in
gear, work seemingly all the time to support the
brood, be kind and never rude, pray from time to
time, and never steal or cheat or commit a crime
and vote your conscious, neither red nor blue
watch out cowboy
you can get shut out of this democracy

your voice tuned into but a gasp
canceled, is the term they use
for anyone who fails to tow the ideological line
you will be a racist, if you fail to see a structural base
for it all, meaning you're one too, knowing you are not
just doesn't matter

the elite of a new orthodoxy they have created to
get and hold power, need not be true and is mostly
false, no matter
atone for white privilege, on your knees, you're a homophobe
you flag waving, God fearing, Star Spangled Banner singing
populist, SOB

better speak up while you can
the chokehold is about to be closed and
all the other unsophisticated "common"
men silenced
tolerance is gone, civility crushed, coercion reigns
what's on your mind suppressed, as they strangle our freedoms
to death.

Where Have All the Axes Gone

The Magna Carta rests behind glass
chewed on by a rat, commemorating that time
rebellious barons told King John that they mattered
too, not just his divine right to do whatever
he desired, then in 1215

and in time, the King of England, Scotland and
Ireland put up with a Parliament that limited some
powers, mostly of the taxes collected that enabled them to
war with France and Spain, and make all there spurious
claims

They all believed from one line of monarchs to another
That they had a direct line upstairs and were entitled to
Decide what everyone should do, until they so irritated the
Parliament, after being shut down for years, that they eventually
got removed

So it came to pass on Charles the First, who thought himself above the
people
Always and Parliament for almost a dozen years
They voted execute the dude one Tuesday in January 1649
He wore two shorts so he would not shake

In the winter wind, and appear weak to the people
He thought had no right to deny his direction
The axe came from due from a skilled executioner
Taking his head from body with one swipe, held he head
To the mob, who gasped, and let out a collective sigh
And unusually, someone sewed back his head
before the burial rite

Roundheads came and went
Cromwell running a country without a King
And it went poorly, more admonitions to be
truly puritanical, until the old man died
and the King returned
Charles again, the second
Who was "merry" was the claim
suffered through the last bubonic plague
killed 7,000 a day, and then London caught fire
as he played away in court, knocked up 13 mistresses
all the while tracking down the men who signed
his father's death warrant
when they found them, some were strangled
hung alive, castrated, and burned
revenge for a righteous axe

No More Dalai Lama's

Will the world be the same
or lost even more
if reincarnation stops in a
room in Dharamshala
when he gets to 90, the
Dalai Lama that is, who has been
the incarnate one, since they found him
In 1937, at two, Lhamo Thondup
And the seers all knew, he was to become
Tenzin Gyatso, the 14th of them since
Gedun Drupa in 1391
Possessed of kindness, wisdom, and
The ability to see past the here and now
It what should be the future anyhow

But after, being pursued by the Chinese
Like Chiang Kai Chek and certainly Chairman Mao
Who didn't want him around to display his
presence in the face of their oppression
blasting temples, and exploding Tibetans
across the high terrain
enough of evil forces in full display to
make even the most transcendent being

want to say, its time to just go away

no more source of lightness of being
no more filter of darkness turned into light
no more chuckle and harmony surrounded by
dark tones and screams from injustices
running through his psyche on humid, Indian
nights

even DL can have enough
the Lama has served his time
over 600 years to roam and come again
offering consistent joy, focus, and depth
each and every time

Tenzin Gyatso is most popular and
Modern as well
Dispensing wisdom on Twitter, Facebook
And even Instagram
A digital man
Bringing mountaintop to everyplace
Insight to everyman
But wondering if some of him has reached
Any one of us

No one listens
Inside their silos, seeing only what they
Want to see, being what they see
Captured in insularity
Taking selfies encouraging narcissism

And a philosophy of nothing, but not his nothingness
Just an anger of what is and what they
Wannabe
Nihilism as some grand ideal

It is his call, the provenance of no one else
Whether to reincarnate or wary of the Chinese
Creating their own, version, supple, and serene
About what they see as true
Better, perhaps, to end it, this line of
wise and subtle men who with a phrase can
damn the most powerful and autocratic of men
and just let go, which is the Buddhist way,
attached to nothing
seeking nothing more than the present moment
and not expecting the promise of the next

The Bastards Cut The Eucalyptus Tree

It is not a cataclysm or a revelation
that you get accustomed to where you are
Even if you yearn to be another place with
broad vistas out your screen door and not
a line of cars and Marines on Kawasaki's
roaring by at 3am on their way to a shift at
Camp Pendleton

I could lay in bed and gaze a sturdy tree
50 feet tall, that would shed its skin occasionally
and smell of its oils
surrounded by other shrubs and such
blocking out the boys across the way
who spent most nights
dancing with tank topped girls and
playing drinking games, laughing hardy
until they collapsed on weekend nights
all knocked out, but mostly out of sight

Orange cones laid down
by Spanish speaking Juan's and Raul's
when I left just at dawn
they pulled the chain saw into motion

the buzz of it, I could hear as I pulled away
no one ever thinks the damage to be done
will be to you, always the other guys world
not yours,
that's what gets you through, always, about
them not you

blinds closed, the alteration unrevealed
when I rise at dawn and open them to
see what the weather might be
nothing blocks my view, sawdust and branches
spewed, what was once a sturdy tree, sawed into
eleven sections, on the ground askew
not a damn thing I can do
the bastards just changed my point of view
the hummingbirds are gone, but they where
they must go
where will I?

Eight Dollars and Some Change

That's it in my right pocket
until Friday
back to five bucks a day
just enough gasoline to get back and
forth on the freeway, three lights away

worn wallet once full of
presidential faces, Washington's mostly
a Jefferson or two, three Jackson's gone
to fuel the car 3.79 @gallon, and me with
crap that passes for a nibble or a meal
frozen outside of Abilene until liberated
in my ancient microwave
and a stop for the shirts from Jesus
even though I was on third round on the
ones I had, I went by each week to give
him 30 bucks, so he could survive

not a new path, cashless mid-week fright
eaten a single orange and a pack of graham crackers
before
trolled free happy hour buffets
when they existed

resigned myself to a generic box of Frosted Flakes
for a week, milk less, floating in tap water
dipping stale, burnt toast in a half a can of
minestrone

not so much a strain to get through
from one day to another hunger
comes and goes, as long as you know
cash is coming and regularity is on the
way

when you have eight bucks and some change
and can't put your wits away
the big picture loses its focus, everything else
fades
who gets to sleep in the White House
live in the space station
line up first for some inoculation
pass along something to the next generation

just buy the big box of sugar covered flakes
a 1.39 cherry pie, and the largest orange you can find
at Moe's gas station, where he has a few in store
call it a dinner for a night or two
and show some damn gratitude that this is
the only deprivation, and a few deep breaths
will get you through, the next ten days

There Will Always Be Critics

Bloated intellectuals
Bloviating incessantly, enamored
By their own corpulence of words
Polluting hemispheres of thought
With random electrons tossed as
spears towards any heart determined to
provide something meritorious as frivolous
as humor or as grave as an essential truth

puffy faces as though extracted from the Seine
doughy torsos hiding rib and bone
capped teeth to assure a Vampire's bite
a joint in her purse
an oxy or two in his pocket to take the
edge off the essential pain of what they really
do

some are paid to offer a point of view
of this painting, or architecture, or just
to scan the cultural milieu
ex post facto slaps from Broadway to the MET
never rising to the nth degree of merit
always seeing something in decline, offering

warning, distain, and forced humility on anything
that might put a buck in an artists pocket

always there to testify
"Hey, is that a horse, on the cave wall?"
"are you kidding me"
Monet lacked clarity
Picasso was unhinged
Modigliani was stuck on long necked women
Rothko created outside his limits
Basquiat was derivative
Bernstein full of schlock
Pavarotti just a populist and
Beyonce, Megan Thee Stallion, Cardi B
Hardly worthy of a column inch
Assassins of dreams
Applying choke holds on creation
Poisoning recipes of ideas, letting blood
From those that do, anything beyond their
Grasp, that has a chance to last,
Transcend, elevate, motivate, and stir
The spirit that they would deter from rising, to satisfy their inner demons

Send Me a Muse

Everyone gets lost and comes up dry of
Thought and inspiration
Nothing flows forth of any real value
sucked out mind, dormant, useless noise,
empty, a nothingness without karmic virtue
occupied with mundane concerns
putting nothing down, hitting delete
the crumpled paper of today, no nails driven
canvas stroked in color, marble chipped away
hymn hummed, symphony created

stillness, undesired respite
staring at Hemingway's White Bull
ferocious blankness there
white on white saying not a thing
not a Supreme statement by Kaz Malevich
ahead of his era in 1916

Zeus gave the world nine of them
His daughters each a muse
Became a shepherd to woe
Mnemosyne, of Titan progeny
The keeper of memory, broad shouldered

Square jawed, over six foot, a veritable tower
of sinew and mass, which she had to be to
sustain nine one night stands, back to back
where Zeus impregnated her all nine times
then retreated after they came to be raised
by Apollo just the same

Clio for history, Erato for love poetry, Euterpe for music,
Melpomene for tragedy, Polyhymnia for sacred verse,
Terpsichore for dance, Thalia for comedy
And the most powerful of all
Calliope who had the most melodious tones
Two women challenged her to a contest of the
Voice expressed, she beat them down, and ended their
Quest to best her, as she turned them into magpies

All statuesque, voluptuous, inspiring goddesses
That would merely appear, and send your mind into
High gear, send me mother or anyone, a muse from
Anywhere, to lift me from indolence and creative
Despair to the banks of a river where ideas still flow
And the muses dance unclothed

King Tide Come and Low Tide Go Me With the Treacherous Undertow

For werewolves and their pretenders
full moons are transformative
evil emerges as fog enshrouds a darkened night

some drip into existence in pouring rain
walking through a burning field of sugar cane
cracking open heads and eating uncle Tom's
brain

nightmares come, never really leave a psyche
scarred by thoughts of running away from a terrible
something, that you cannot escape, sheets soaked
as your own scream awakens you
on a tortured night

before the sun, sidewalks flood, sandbags soak
as the King Tide rises
dogs splash as day breaks
beautiful this fall

526 in '54

Not easy to run the table in straight pool
I don't care how good you think you are
When there is money on it, and just the two
of you, its not a movie with Gleason and Newman,
who by the way, had never even held a pool cue
before the movie came

I was all of eleven when my Popa Joe
recounted to me in our bedroom that we shared
How his buddy Joe's son, Willie in '54, in actual exhibition
Competition ran 526 balls over two days in March
at the old East High Billiard Club in Springfield, Ohio
he showed me a Xerox of the affidavit, that he signed
along with 34 other guys who saw it
sent there by his father Joe to watch over the
younger Mosconi

at six Willie was beating the Philly sharks
standing on a box, cleaning up the dough
for his father who owned the joint, and after
hours the old man and my Pops played until
dawn, mostly straight pool until dawn

when they raced to the nine ball
and then they cracked some eggs with
Willie and smoked a long Cuban

Before, I really played any ball
there was pool, surrounded by old men
who that game, and a bit about life
treated me with grace, never cursed
or spit, when I was in the parlor
and Pops always threw me outside when they
fought, hooted and howled

I grew up fast in that bedroom I shared
The weight of the world entered there
and playing a game for stakes taught me something
too about being good at what you do, because
in the end you can't fake a shot, and you better
run true, or all that bluff and bravado will
sink as fast as a misguided cue, into a corner
pocket.

Beating the Crap Out of America

I don't go out much anymore
That rutted path to work
Reaching for frozen food packaged in Oklahoma
The runs that offer solace and preserve what is
left of my sanity

rarely sit, pondering,sipping
an expensive cup of Joe
until a cold, rainy Sunday arrives
and I'm leaving the gym, after a morning
on the big black bag
roll into Howard's ubiquitous place
and get a Venti for 2.45

across from me, a trifecta of commentators on the
American scene, at 8:45 am, a verbal essay on where, what
we are and what we ought to be
here's that litany:
systemically racist
sexist, full of misogyny
bigots in power
violent against people of color
xenophobic (if poorly defined)

anti- immigrant
without gratitude to the people of color
deny us reparations
statues must be eradicated
never really emancipated
capitalism is taboo
socialism makes sense too
from each according to his ability to each
according to her need

enough venom over a half hour
to
launch a series of revolts, fuel a protest,
inflame a mob, lynch most of us for the
errors of time past, and cancel culture,
morality, all of Western civilization until the
new man/woman emerges and remains

I want to go over there and play Socrates
offer up Euripides, Aristotle's Golden Mean,
review James Baldwin, celebrate Langston Hughes,
lionize, Thurgood Marshall, or applaud Si se puede
embrace Chavez and Dolores Huerta's rise
but I turned page A 28 of the Sunday Times
on my way devoted to get through it all by
ten, hoping the rain ended by then

they seemed happy as they left
the Algonquin club of the coffee shop
lives to live, in this Amerika, they seemed to

detest, had still offered them such freedom
to overtly protest
and beat the crap of all it is, through a looking glass
distorted by their youth, clouded by anger, that
like the windshield of their Mercedes, you could not
see anything with clarity, unless you turned on the
wipers

Good reason to not stop by
Pretend you're reading the NYT
Which has the same viewpoint from page to page
cornered I am taking body blows on a grey Sunday
protecting my head from the beating
as my ribs are broken for no apparent reason

Too Many UGB's

"The bitch hit me with a toaster"
Bill Murray as Scrooge snarled away
at Carole Kane in good witch attire
playing the ghost of all things
Xmas present

So encumbered and encased by
a monumental ego, it would
more than a toaster to the end to rock him
into awareness that he was big time, master of
the universe spewing venomous scum
with every utterance and action

such presumption, by the presumptuous is
hardly uncommon, possessing some uniqueness
of voice, look, command, dress, vanity or all of
the above, they exist a few steps above the rest of
us elevated by something apparent, allowing the
separation from anyone else's
moral code

they rarely say thank you and mean it
will never go out of their way to say Merry Xmas
expect you to minister to them, hold an umbrella over them
on 42nd street in a pouring spring rain, and take the cab
you hailed

laugh when they are comical
smile at their every whim
put aside your private hour so they
can better schedule the shopping after
Thanksgiving

You see them everywhere pushing
around the most and rest of us
who have no obvious special thing that
cuddles our self image and blows bubbles
up our ass, so when they fart it never
has aroma

Louie at the fish market called them
Ungrateful bastards, a tribe of UGB's
He'd point them out after wrapping fish
For them or more likely their drivers and
Maids
"There's another member of the tribe,
another mother UGB, where the hell do they
all come from "he would say
wiping the blood away, on his white apron
turned bright red by noon

Like to take a filet knife to them
Open up their insides, and see what it is
That makes them better than me.

Saving George Bailey

I cry still after all these years
when George Bailey walks towards the bridge's edge
in the driving snowstorm, ragged, forlorn
and lost, convinced he is that everyone will be
better off, if he is just gone
and Frank Capra has his camera show the
teeming river below
still George moves on towards a decided
end

Then Clarence appears, jolly and sweet
quiet but determined to save this one
lost soul
and the tears come here, knowing all the rest
intimately, empathic deep down from being there, that feeling of the
only way to quiet the noise and end the chaos
is to exit

it does not take much to enter the room of utter despair
where what you thought you would become
what you could achieve
who you loved would love back
people would listen to your thoughts

respect your point of view
run through most of life not mocked and berated
occasionally even elevated by the good you might
have done
the bad buried, and the good of you survived

just one or two crossroads where
you chose the path best taken
stayed silent rather than mouthed off
acted with courage, and had no cowardice to
bear, when you were most needed
you were there
you know perfection exists for a chosen few
and talent is also rare
but having none of it should not lead to
abject despair
there is always another sunrise, somewhere
Clarence knows and shows George
the righteous way
there will always be bells ringing and angels
to save souls, in the movies of long ago and
every tear, reminds me of that as the years pile high

The Man in the Next Seat to Wilmington

There is a high speed train that takes men in
jackets and ties to the corridors of power
in D.C.
Faces stern going in and relaxed, if worn
coming back, those after something like me
and those who say, yes and no, like that
guy with a generous smile, one seat
away from me, who I always see on the
way back south
I get off at 30th street, he at Wilmington
with a pleasant disposition, who always
nodded at me and flashed his whites
and introduced himself one quiet night

he was a junior senator to a guy I knew
Dick Roth, and told me, he rode the rail
every night, so he could tuck in his boys
at night, and I left it there, unexplored
for a good long while, until a gal I knew

rode along and told me a narrative
of woe
he gets elected at 29.9, awaits to be sworn when
he turns 30, stays in D.C., while his wife and kids
pack in a station wagon to go buy a Xmas tree
then he gets a call, a trucks hits them all
wife and daughter gone
two boys alive and broken
he wants to walk away
but stays, a grit that comes from where
only he can know

Big Mike Mansfield back in the day
swears him in during the boys hospital stay
and he agrees to give it six months to see, if
he can hack it all
"we can always get another Senator"
he famously would say,
"but the boys can't get another father"

I always nodded as he passed into that
seat, not knowing how a man goes on
finds his way, and stays on course
becomes a man of consequence and contribution
through remorse and despair

and when he holds up his hand to say

"I swear to uphold…."

I think all who know him would simply say

Way to go, Joe, way to go

And finally let this warhorse lead the way

Moon Over the Bay

Why is it so difficult to get outside
Of your petty misery on any given day
Let go of it all, play at being carefree
Tell the furies to stop whining
forget the rent is due, the refrigerator
empty, and you are deep inside many
shades of darkest blue

tide out, hard sand ahead
fire pits, burning broken pallets
with covens of people around them
tribal throwback now looking out at
a metropolis, that just turned on its
lights
and a moon rises nearly full

paints the water with its light
alone in the sky tonight
Mars once there by it just days
before, rushed to see it just that way
not knowing if 23 years from now, I will
be around to see it again
orange sunset yields to indigo sky

moon follows as I circumnavigate the
bay, each step pushing the concerns of
now away

then, remarkably, I construct a prayer
and offer it, mostly of thanks not want
direction over gifts, a guiding hand
to find some worthy path
gaze back at the fires, the city lights
the cold black sand
and put my hands together in a prayers
embrace

tears come, not an exaggeration of what
I feel inside, of wanting to know and not
Knowing what is always next

I exit the moon's light into a
darkened field, step in a pile
of crap from a couple's Dobermans
and laugh

The Stop Sign is 100 Yards Away

Wolfman has a pacemaker
he looks like Lou Albano
who wore a rubber band in his goatee
Howled like DJ Wolfman Jack
Retired to Naples so he could play Hemingway
And grumble at the sea, and grill his catch
on warm winter nights
started building houses to pass the time
until the old bones began to fall away
knees replaced, a busted hip, a shoulder
now displaced
nothing slowed him much
until the pump went erratic and the scopes
and dyes revealed he needed a stent and
a pacemaker to tick tock his day to day
until, he just wears out
slumping over like Fredo out in a boat
on Biscayne Bay

all the boys now men who bled with me
on fields of grass and mostly dirt
as we exited adolescence, with bruises and rashes
gashes, and scars that never healed made it to the

last act, with that ultimate stop sign
coming closer, only 100 yards away
everyone of us, finally slowing down taking our
heavy foot off the life accelerator, as though
it will delay the arrival at the destination
as though we control that anyway

Cosmo has COPD
Big Mike gave up a leg to diabetes
Augie lost his hair and had his neck fused after his
pick up hit a tree in 2003
Arnie has aplastic anemia and sits with Doris
as platelets are transfused

Lonnie looks young for his age
Lifts weights in the driveway every afternoon
Fern drives him around, he mostly can't remember
Where he is, or who, and doesn't know her name

Blackjack who stopped working young
After the lotto came his way
Is getting his estate together knowing
pancreatic cancer will put the brakes on
his field of play

They all see that stop sign
The warning lights are flashing on the
Dashboard of their lives
Not for me
I imagine it distant, behind these

Mountain passes, out there fog shrouded
Too much to cover, so much undone
More stops where something of merit
Might be done, everything avoided or left out
found, and memory retrieved

with no other infirmity but time passing
a will to go on outdone by the pure reality that
brings a man to exhaustion by a life done
running on fumes anyway for the last hundred miles
ready to stop, be chopped into shards, discarded
and recycled, perhaps, in the universe at large

Gotta Stay Ahead of the Wave

Men go through the days deluded
Acting as though they are in charge
Of what used to be called destiny, a concept rarely
Offered up in the modern day,
So certain that what they do and say is
Just fine and o.k.
Even though there is no master plan or
Direction at all, mostly, just
Whatever happens is what there is
No existential play, no Kant or Aristotle
No Golden Mean to find, no grail to seek
Not even a rumpled, well used,roadmap
of how to manage
a well lived life, stuck in the hip pocket
of well worn pair of jeans

You do not require Freud or Jung
Sartre, Aurelius, or even Tony Robbins
to tell you that the examined life is more likely
to get you what you want from cash, to sex to
even some measure of happiness, fleeting though
it may be
or old Holtz, Lombardi in his prime,

the eternal righteousness of Wooten
to know it is a disciplined life that is worth living
not the unplanned, non directed, indulgent
one that responds to genetic switches and instincts
suggesting lizard and ape mimed minds

here's the three you can control,
what you think, your view of things, that outlook
is all yours
what you say, utterances each time you offer them,
define you in everyway
Can you get through a sentence without an expletive display
Be quiet when you might otherwise have your views
Offered to just declare, you exist today
What you consume, is number tres'
What you shove in your mouth to fuel your multi- layered
Cell array, or just to fill some hole, of anger, grief, loss, or
Incapacity, or to avert boredom, support indolence, delay
action, until the time for it passes away
and what you take in your mind, is it diversion from all the platforms of
play and porn, or do you seek substance so your intellect can be
reborn?

Because, if what you can control you do not
And you fritter away the dialogue you can control
Between you and you, when the forces comes
You will be carried to their shores, if not drown

They come like waves, of sizes vast and not
That taken to shore late will break you

But ridden, surfed, ahead of each break can
Elevate, exhilarate, empower you to ride
fearlessly, seemingly without effort, with a grace
that comes from diligence, preparation, and
exploration of your purpose and the reclamation
of your soul

Gotta get ahead of the forces
Ride the waves of adversity
Wake up
Mind the way, watch what you say,
Don't let what life you are given just
Drift away.

Warm Winter Wind

Blows the newspaper pages
That only I seem to read anymore
Stacked high on this concrete table
Running through them, ripping out
Articles and entire pages, to read carefully
Later, after the sun sets and the December
chill returns

cost as much as a small book these
Sunday papers, mostly recaps of all the
Conflicts over who gets what, who gets pushed aside,
What dame is in flames over her lost or abusive
paramour
What politician is being finally shown the exit door
To a theater where he cried 'fire' once too often
Sports don't matter seen it all on the phone
Bet whatever line I chose, and did it all without the
prose

Cloudless sky matches the eyes of a tall redhead
In a thong, on all fours, writing something, intensely
on a yellow pad, she of twenty some years, as much
an anachronism writing, as I am reading a paper

her ass pristine, untouched, reddened by the
wind, oblivious she is to one O.G.
attempting to keep the pages from blowing away
and using them as a prop to keep my eyes down
and not get caught in the old man's stare

warm winds stir a nascent libido
encourage reverie that we might
converse over what she is writing and I
am reading
until I close my eyes and feel the breeze
hear the papers rustle, knowing nothing
happens here, ever
and she stands triumphantly, throws down her pen
and lavishes lotion on her arm
I glance at the Op-Ed on getting troops out
of Afghanistan
catch a notion of déjà vu
put my hands over my eyes
and shake my head

No Argument Here

It was October, 1858, Lincoln and
Douglas finished their seventh debate
enough wind expended to satisfy both of them
one got 60 minutes, the other 90 to rebut
and then another 30 for good measure
Folks could sit and listen, then, with not
much else to do on a fall afternoon in
Alton, Illinois

Slavery was the topic, mostly and each had a
Distinct and unambiguous point of view
They tore at the arguments, and offered their view
of what was once called the 'truth of things'

A goddess rules all dialogue today
Eris, she is called
The purveyor of chaos, the unsettled and
Dismay
Arguments that come from her are only meant
To splay the other side, savage their position
And offer nothing more than argument as counterpoint
The damn, whole truth doesn't matter

A time long gone, now when
Arguments were offered to get to the
crux and find a way to solve a problem
and not delay
crushed by the display of arguments without
purpose, but to decay the other side
and never seek resolve

thesis met anti-thesis
synthesis would ensue, one result
to another out of compromise would do
and evolution would bring progress to the
cultural milieu

such Hegelian structure
firm a foundation as it might be
is lost in a debate without dialogue
that sets truth aside, for an endless
night of argument that just will not subside
as no argument moves us forward
no higher ground is near, stuck in the filth of arrogance
where the 'truth of things' is smothered

Waiting on a Sidewalk

For a traffic light to change
Not a thought of anything more
Than getting back on the bicycle
Lay out twenty more miles on a
Straight line out of the city
To a hot shower and a bowl of
Steel cut oatmeal and blue berries

At yellow on its way to red, a tricked out
Subaru oversteers, brushes a Ford 150
That slides a short 20 feet in a second
Over a curb
Breaks both knees, crushes a hip, the rib cage
On the way to his neck and flattens his face
Crushing his skull
Leaving the 77 year old dead, after the seconds
of pain and a flash of consciousness
before the end came

accidents happen the cops say
drivers are undamaged which always
seems the way
whatever his life contained whether

substantial, consequential enough to mark his
above ground stay
or a man passing through doing his best to
be sane, responsible, just, and not let
the darkness inside, emerge to harm anyone
but himself

certainly a landing without notice
a blind sided blow of the extreme
the phrase often utilized in jest between
men past their prime
"Doc says I'm healthy as a horse, an organ donor
Unless you're hit by a truck"
Whatever he did or gave
Offered, from gifts given
Sorrow overcome, lives touched by his
Admonitions, perfect smile and still sky blue
eyes
taken, unplanned, in a frenzy of miscalculation
forcing flesh and steel to mesh
sending a soul standing on a corner
waiting for a light to change
on a road trip to eternity

In an Archway on 72nd at 10:50 40 Years Ago Tonight

A fan waits with a :38
Yoko exits the limo then John
Five shots, four in Lennon's back
'I'm shot, I'm shot"

The shooter takes off his jacket
Puts down the gun, and sits reading
Catcher in the Rye
Cops put John in the back seat of
The black and white
So much blood, they cannot stop
No ambulance in sight

Sirens howl in Midtown
radios blare in bodegas
cab drivers stand in clusters listening
and talking loud
spontaneity springs from curiosity
crowds come to the Dakota
and Roosevelt Hospital where he
cannot survive, so shattered inside
his eloquence a legacy, his purity defiled

when asked if he is John Lennon he can only
sputter, "Yeah"

Men don't struggle with memory of such
fateful nights, epiphanies come later, except for
Pearl Harbors, and 9/11's, that compel some men
to sign up for a fight
You know who you were with
What bed you occupied that night
Whether you went to work or slept through the night
Rarely did anything change for you, at least right away
Where there resolutions made, or did you just go
on that day, another well known bloke taken away
by some twisted, insane, lost SOB, who will
spend his sorry life in prison, and rejected when he
comes for parole 11 times
That night fades, but the forty years do not
Of your life of love, loss, and the vagaries of any life
Consequential or not
What have you done with those years, since
John and Yoko walked under that arch on 72nd at 10:50 pm, on that chilly December night

So Who Are You Dating

The still married guy always asks
No one, I always say, not on my field of
Play, maybe again someday
When my patience returns for endless
verbal foreplay, the hours of semantics,
good listening habits and a studied look
of interest in all that she may say
just to have some in and out between the silences
that comes with being alone

the few I have attempted were horrible extensions
of a flawed personality that preferred a Novocain
injection for a pending root canal to a luncheon on
some sunny rooftop place with the 50 something
brunette with a flawless complexion and enough
décolletage to harbor a Navy ship
the dental procedure was painful but of determinate
duration

Truthfully, I never had the requisites to entice or charm
a women to the desired conclusion, certainly not now,
where mere creature needs are off most lists, or way past number

ten most wanted things
not a good listener, small talker, dog lover
or walker, could not flirt, show interest in their
great kids climb to high position, amazing grandchildren,
or the new car acquisition, or
the reason for the break ups, his distaste for her growth and
interests, his bad manners, mouth, and choices, his girlfriends
age and disposition
a litany of sorrows, missed opportunities, juxtaposed to the
currency of dreaming again, and being free to be, what she
could not, those decades incarcerated in a slowly dying
marriage

And I had not much to offer to her here
unwilling to play out my own dreary and obvious
story of the reduction of passion, followed by desire
dampened by life, as it is lived from infatuation, to
children, loss and triumph, defeats piled high, accumulating a
mountain of disappointments
none of it offered or required
but if this be dating
I'll pass

Rather take an aspirin or not
pant over some pornographic rot
read In Search of Lost Time on the crapper
for two winter months
wash the car at 3 am
just sit and watch the sun rise, and take an

electronic sabbatical for a full day
all of it more satisfying than the path taken
to get laid, which is not happening anyway

So I often ask, with arrogance in tone
"I'm not dating, Joey, read any good books lately"
And the phone rings, its Lorraine
"Yeah I'd like to see you again, too"
"call you, soon, ok?"
Yeah that will happen
Right.

You Are Not Your Pain

Can you sit on a concrete bench
warmed by winter sun
gulls winging so close they touch your hair
tide pools emerge as the king tide retreats for the
afternoon
everyone muffled to hush tones and in awe
and still cry before it all?

Not tears of loss but of courage
The kind that children have when
They are faced with unbearable circumstances
Except for them
They just go on
Through chemo, spinal taps, hair loss,
Vomiting, needle pain, tubes becoming
Part of them, everything they were
Transformed by some undeserved, unwarranted
Genetic malady, brought on by some switch
They had no hand in, did not desire or contemplate

And, yet they just hold on, even smile
at normal things, a sister's gaff, a brother's
laugh, a father's attempt at humor, a video

game victory, in some imagined battle

when pain comes they are mostly quiet,
even calm, it may appear
a mature knowing that it will rise and to be
with it, embrace it, and eventually it will end
the spasms of pain lessening over time
more life to live in between the hammer lock
it puts on them

the cracked ribs, the distorted collar bone,
the chronic bad knee, the pre arthritic neck, now
arthritic so it turns left not right, ingrown toenails,
throbbing old teeth that still remain, morning razor
cuts, dry eyes, colon without much peristalsis, over active
prostrate, and a memory that loses more every day
are ashamedly not worth further contemplation
or whining into a unfilled space, where the only listener is you

Can you just sit with a boy of eleven
Without his hair, with a Hickman device in his chest
Allowing the doctors chemo access more not less
And watch him eat his green Jello
With a Santa on top in whipped cream
And not cry, there and then as he smiles
Offering the deepest thought any august
philosopher might say
"I have pain, for sure. But, you know,
I am not my pain"

The Commute

I run through the routine
Up as the sky turns from dark to light
Before the sun warms my face
Make my bed, one thing I can control
Before the day unfolds
Mix toothpaste and peroxide and brush
Gargle, as though it will ward off evil matters
Sit in the hope that the colon will awaken

Dress in shorts and worn shoes
Run four miles or so
Forty minutes no matter what the mood
Without a thought
Moving mediation the masters say

Shower, shave fast, ready to go
Somewhere, but, now with nowhere
Without destination, wondering why I
Am not more elated, about something
Always contemplated

How I despised the commute no matter
How glorious and important the job

The commute always brought to dismay
As I attempted to traverse the up and back
Of each damn day

Drive to 30th street station, get on the Amtrak
Train, chat up the astonishingly smashing career girls
Or more likely sit with a man of garlic smell from a meal
The night before at Palumbo's in South Philly
Then the walk across town, through concrete canyons
Everyone with a grayish hue, a scowl and mood to match

Or that drive from Westchester, before the divorce, over
the Bronx River Parkway, onto the parkway, jammed, with
lights, or any alternative on the 95, just as bad on most
nights
Except in Marathon months when I might run from Bronxville
To Central Park, towel off, and take a cab to work, and the train
Home

Whether green lines to Government Square from Newton
In snow storms that ran into April
By rice and soy fields, when I would fall asleep, and wind up
in water up to the windows, saved by farmer Dyson and his tractor
the exact same route for eight years, only way in or out
getting up at 4:30 to drive from LA to Diego, for a 7 am call
or 17 years, in 15 minute sprints at 80, the Indianapolis 500
a few thousand times

No matter what I did
Deep breaths, sing Hari Krisnah, wail Nessun Dorma

Turn up Metallica's Nothing Else Matters
Doo Op, Duke of Earl, The Pyramids Along the Nile,
Be uplifted by Tony Robbins, attempt to learn Mandarin
Text some dumb ass remark to the office mate in pain
Or just go silent, in an effort to not go insane

And it seemed a burden
On reflection it was not
Nothing more than another signal
I am here, today, alive, relevant in some
Small measure, atomized, but still
There on the road or train to somewhere
And now… what

Clear Headed

Without a thought, consideration, worry
or obtuse contemplation
rare it is and comes without willfulness
emerges blank, white on white
the mind a canvas, usually a crowded landscape,
various hues of pastels, and somewhere, always
a darkened night
not this morning

never like this
no gnawing motivation to change the
world's direction
tinker with a thought and mold into
an action
to scramble up the recipe of serenity
of someone else's life
to read a volume dense with unapproachable
prose

unmotivated to do anything
mundane seems monumental
that Everest of laundry remains

untouched
knives, forks, bowls, dishes
of all shapes and designs form a
sculpture in a deserted sink
worthy of Duchampe'
titled, 'Indulence'

every thought that should be there
awaiting activation is lost in a jangle
of a few million, inactivate neurons
odd to have a frontal lobe so clear
that the great unresolved in life
seem nowhere near

After all, I know the
Governor is an imperious, pompous ass
Millions are out of work, and Congress is petrified to act
You can't eat a meal,in or out, 3,000 are dying a day
And the boys at the beach won't wear a mask
Touching is verboten, communication is on a screen,
Castrated by our time, celibate, kiss less, untouched

And on most days I would
Write, speak, opine on it all
But I am clear headed, I see only
What is in front of me, nothing deep
textured,with a perceived revelation

let the world and its dilemmas find another
soothsayer and problem saving maven
no one will care or notice that I've taken one
day off from
worry.

Agent 488- Who Are You?

Before the KGB, CIA, and even 007
there were spies out to crack codes
encrypt enigma machines, resist the Nazi's
in occupied lands, organize resistance,
exploit weak, and evil spirited men from the
evil other sides, all to assist in turning the tide

most unknown and without celebrity
heroic deeds done and lives lost quietly
without fanfare or telegram
not a marker or stone anywhere to lean a
wreath on, or say a prayer to

Mary was a beautiful dame of
The Bancroft family hall of fame
Who owned the Wall Street Journal
She married well, and played the game of Bon
Vivant, played the field in a thoroughly modern style,
Divorced one, picked up another until
The big war came

Became the assistant of a pipe smoking hard ass
On the rise, Allen Dulles, who ran the spy outfit

In Switzerland, called it the Office of Strategic
Services, the OSS, all dark ops, and spycraft
Mary fell for him and she for him, and wartime
Birthed an affair for the duration

"Our romance will cover the work, and our work
Will cover the romance"

And she went on to infiltrate high ranking
filth of Germanic origin
dumping secrets to her beau, and foiling Nazi
plans, as she would go from parlor to bed
on occasion

Mary brought Allen an unlikely agent
Whom she met, when searching for a cure
For her chronic, rapid fire sneezing
A mind master, a pioneer of it,
She stuck him in ritzy hotel room in Lausanne
Got Dulles to stop by and share a pipe bowl
Carl Jung offered his service
to jump into Hitler's mind, and
dissect and predict not only that he would
kill himself sometime soon, but that Germans
could be coaxed back as an ally after the
doom of losing a hideous war

Jung became Agent 488
Sent dispatches now and again
All his insights, in reflection, were spot on

Including his favorite on Hitler
"there is no man inside, he is all shadow
The most evil man I have ever encountered
Who has introspection or remorse"

Dulles went to Agent 488 after the war
As well to help them climb out of that
hell
A man well known enough for walking through
Minds
Was as valuable a spy as any, who carried a
Pipe and a notebook, and nothing else.

Never Play In Any Reindeer Games

Absurd it may be that
Rudolph is not the reindeer he may seem
Bright eyed, smiling champion of Santa on
Xmas day
But rather something else not fanciful, merry,
or part of the Christmas story itself

created by a Jew fighting for all his creativity
to be an all American, not just another first generation
nobody
It came to Robert l. May who created Rudolph for pay
And laid down the poem and a book for a department store chain
Until his brother in law Johnny Marks
turned it into a pleasant enough tune
that Gene Autry could go ahead and croon

turns out it was autobiography
of Johnny's childhood years in Mount Vernon
ostracized, pushed around, laughed at like he was
some clown, all composed Rudolph's plight
on that Xmas eve night

"all the other reindeer used to laugh and
Call him names, they never let poor Rudolph
Play in any reindeer games"

But he preserved, like all the other young Jewish boys
In the suburbs of New York
Didn't change… stayed true to himself, and couldn't help
Glow with his shiny nose… until
acceptance came… and history was made

how odd it might seem now
that this Johnny brought Rudolph to us all
a parable of being an outsider, but never losing
faith, in who you essentially are
and triumphing over it all
soaring is the metaphor
that millions sing each year
universal truths, that never really fade
the legacy of all
who believe in bravery, staying true to yourself
and shining like a beacon through whatever is your
darkest night

What You Miss

Age brings regrets, bottles to
piss in in your car, benign spots
enlargements of once compliant organs
energetic surges and brown outs
your head seems to enlarge
the West Point posture gravitationally
bending down and you can still
hit the big black bag, without the
Marciano zest, Chinese food cascades
off the chopsticks into your lap
and you don't smile that much
although you never did anyway

another February night, moonless
clouded, with hard rain to waken you at
3:10
The ceiling is the screen for the movie going
through your head, entitled
"What you miss" in technicolor

Having a head on my shoulder in bed
Listening to a woman you love snore
The smell of French toast cooking

The taste of maple syrup on anything
Toddlers giggling, and jumping on your bed
A dog that jumps as high as your head when you
come through the front door
your sister's smile, after you haven't seen her
for a while, like years

the girls at Waikiki, the long paddle out to
a breaker for a long surf to shore
jumping from your porch into an aquarium sea
in Moorea
taking all the blue trails on a late winter afternoon
on Vail mountain
running deserted streets in Xinjiang when the sun
never sets
putting a stone on my son's grave in a pouring
winter rain

damp, just cut grass
running in cleats to catch a pass
shaving an unblemished face
the anticipation, exhilaration of that first date
every,single sexual engagement, coitus
the after, mostly
marriage vows, dancing with her mother
trading war stories with the father's
holding babies, anyone's
falling asleep on the couch with one
in your arms

playing the big shot in Atlantic City and Las Vegas
making out under the boardwalk
sleeping there until dawn
the smell of old damp wood
the elation of learning to sail
winning a fistfight and stopping the blood
flow from your broken nose
the warm September ocean at the shore
eating a cheesesteak with wiz, and browned onions

a bright colored fall on the neighborhood trees
trees on streets
neighborhoods, and guys to sit on the stoop with
next door
filthy jokes that were funny then
magazines with naked women in them
Dutchmaster cigars and the gents who smoked them
The cop who saved my ass, and set me straight
Lemon water ice on humid August nights

That hug from her that made the insanity
Seem bearable and alright

Better than counting sheep
What you miss is a long list, more lost than gained
makes a man sleepy fast, just so you can forget the
past, for another night, as the rain plays a melody
that's sweet as a jazz riff ......

Will I Run Fast Again

And pass someone from behind
on streets now, I find, a woman comes
by in stunning latex wrapped around powerful
ass and thighs
moves effortlessly by
as I pick up the pace to stay in play
huffing all the way, she looks back and sighs
as if to say
"you don't have it anymore"

Been down some trails and asphalt places
With a rack of medals marking I was at those races
Middle of the pack, for certain, but there to say
I exist, I am here, today
This linear endeavor I will complete from A to formidable B
And will end it with a grimace, but know at least that I did
Finish

Shivered in Hopkinton in a steady drizzle, up Heartbreak Hill
to the Pru
huddled underneath a shrub at Fort Wadsworth, before shaking
with 30 thousand others across the Verrazano
one time chatted up Ingemar Johansen, far after his prime

ran miles behind Bill Rogers who owned Boston's best time
three loops around the Schuylkill, finished where Rocky would
run up 72 steps years later
stood by bonfires in a red canyon in Utah, where the Milky Way was out
in plain site

went back to the Penn relays as an adult
busted my gut and seared my lungs pretending to be
rejuvenated in a 440 leg, with no devil to trade my soul
watched fireworks go off on Ala Moana before that
marathon, repeated that six times, just to relish the end
jumping into the sea, and pretending I would never come back
again

took on Death Valley on a dare
beat the other old guys, of which there but a few
and once ran around the Liberty Bell only to end
63 miles later on the boardwalk in Atlantic City
With two people there to say
"way to go" when I finally got there 12 hours later

They can't know, these lithe and muscled gals
That I've pounded enough roads to at least register a nod
Nobody cares what came before
No cred exists anymore
What you did, how many starting lines you faced
Daunting distances to endure
Does not matter, to anyone, never did
The only person on earth to ever care was you
"Run until you can't"

Banister would say from
his wheelchair, when asked
the ultimate triumph isn't speed
never was
it is what you can endure, until you can't
anymore....

Curbside Moral Dilemmas

It is a canard and a dodge of the way
The world wags, really
To pretend that the great choices only
Occur
In hallowed halls, the well of the Senate,
Before some pompous judge,
A tribunal, committee of a review,
Dissertation panel of pious professors,
Or that parole board that substitutes
What is correct as the wind blows
Believing in restorative justice for assassins
And deviates, and a few sexual offenders

For those of us living the small
Inconsequential lives, you know, the one
You imagine is elevated by highly righteous choices
But is actually fueled by quiet desperation
When you are convinced you know right from wrong
Until wrong comes with a bonus
of a few extra bucks, or
a free

willing, woman who wants to forget her past
or a fifty yard line pass, for letting Manny
get to see your boss, and kiss her ass

there it is by the gutter
a wallet flayed, as you run towards it
filled with plastic, and the corners of two
hundreds peeking out of its leather embrace
so you pick it up,run with it in your hand
and contemplate moral choice at 6:45 am

a mile or so elapses
the scenarios come and go
take the money
take the money call the owner
call the owner and be a saint for a moment
give the money to the homeless guy by the toilets in the park
toss the wallet
you know what is right, don't you?

Stop by the boats, open it open
Nothing but gift cards, no name on any of the stuff
No license or credit cards, nameless
So far, no high moral dilemma
That hundred isn't real
Its labeled show money, and is ripped in two
Two actual dollars are imbedded, it becomes clear what to do
Put the wallet on the stoop by the water fountain
Rip up the fake Franklin
Take the two and give them to Marty just as he awakes

Run the last miles relieved
That there was no more to do
The right choices made for you
The dilemmas ahead that day would not
be as easy to kick to the curb

Horseradish Memories

When you are alone
memories come unprompted by only
that inner voice, shouting, snarling
at times whispering for your attention
Proustian the lit boys would say
That transports you in a zetosecond
To a scene so vividly depicted in your cortex
Every part of it is present, and real

And it freezes you in a moment you may cherish, fear
or could not stand to live again
as you open a prepared jar of horseradish of beet
color, to spread on your gefilte fish
pretending a family was there, the dead returned
and the living by your side
and you dip a fork of fish into it and it is too much
as it was when you were a boy, your sinus cavities
ablaze, eyes watered
and everyone laughed, an excuse to sip the sweet grape
wine, and watch Uncle Usher toast your discomfort
with his plum liquor, at 110 proof

before the next engagement, you

see your grandmother on the stoop at that
South Philly row house, three marble steps
And a grater, that I held for her as she pulled the
Horseradish across it, with remarkable vigor for an old
woman with gnarled hands, sinew everywhere, who
hummed some ancient tune, until the radish was gone
into an old pan, pure white heat, awaiting consummation

she would laugh when it was done, take another one
have me sample a forkful, to see if I would tear, and I never
failed the test, and she would pull my head to her and
kiss my forehead, and wave to her sister on the stoop across the
narrow street, signaling the world was in its place
at least the horseradish was done

as though the world could just stop
the impossible journey to get to this place, unspoken
it was enough, there were grandchildren,
a family in good health
and the Cossacks were not coming at dawn

Knucksie

on the mounds of diamonds
from Sheepshead Bay to Bridgeport, Ohio
South Philly to Braddock
Every young phenom threw hard
and fast, until the sun went down
arms of steel, joints fluid and tendons
that seemed to last forever
more strikes than balls from each
adolescent spring until late fall

so it was for Phil and Joe
a coal miners boys, who pitched for
solace, and fresh air, had a fast ball
as good as most, but knew something
his rivals avoided
taught him from a wise old miner

the heat gets cool
the arm wears out
the shoulders and tendons lose
their spring
elbows get dipped in ice and
what once was too fast to see

will come in slo mo to the lefty
with two guys on base, and one hit away
from a win
so he taught his boys, and Phil exceeded
at something he called the knuckler
that had its own spin
even the catchers had to get bigger gloves
to handle the damn thing

years passed from club to club
wins piled up
at 318, 3,342 strike outs
even threw a shutout at 46 years of age
record stood for 25 years
only threw the knuckleball to the last batter
struck him out

Niekro threw his way into the Hall
of Fame, Knucksie, in quotes on his plaque
kids take their ball and gloves out after a visit and
attempt to throw the pitch to their dads
who know that its more than a trick to know
you need more than one fast pitch to get through
a career, in anything, even the best hard and fast
guys slow, and only the wise, and crafty know
that sometimes it pays to be slow, with a change up
or,even, a knuckleball to throw
to baffle the big batters, who are out to
knock you on your ass, and hit your ball out of the
park.

The Pioneer Takes the Arrows

Whenever I go to read some guy will
Always ask
"Hey, Kemo is that all true?"
And I pause wanting to say all that follows
But mostly don't and reply with a smile
If I can raise one on cue
"Mostly, Mostly, True, in most places
To fill the spaces"

Poetry has its own truth
It ensues from within you, reflux
of images, and thoughts, brought up
from your enteric mind, bile and
acids, if it hurts to write it down
romance, devotion and ego
if it emerges from your cerebral cortex
in full flower

sometimes it just flashes out of you
a jumble of impulses from reptile,
brain, all limbic, defensive, aggressive,
angry, sexy, with wood to show for it
slithers onto the page, unrepentant

unedited, dangerous recollections

what of it true
all of it dude
conflations, imaginations, permutations
of something once real or felt
with open heart, and burdening you
to be expressed before it severs an artery

we are on a journey to find ourselves
that stops off at our soul
trailblazers of insight, down rutted roads
cluttered by everything, we hoped for or ever wanted
totaled by the crackups and accidents of our lives

The pioneers get the arrows as they
Go along their way not knowing what they'll
Uncover or find, but brave enough to say
Its' all mostly true, and I'd do it anyway

58,220 KIA
551,232 pieces on Phu Tho Stadium Floor

Nothing is congruent, falls into
obvious patterns and designs, what once seemed
orderly and cause with effect, once sublime
shattered by reality stochastic by design
nothing sums up, makes sense, random
in ascendance, logic beaten to a pulp
good results and justice hoped for a long
forgotten shipwreck

a neighborhood of young men
lost in that distant jungle war
names on black slate, better than just a lonely grave
wedged into a civil war, fragged by all sides
all taken horribly, removed in body bags
a destiny, result undeserved, pieces on a generals
map, on a journey to somewhere, a living hell
with no way back

Imagine then, in old Saigon, now Ho Chi Minh City
1600 economic students, whose fathers' fought for them
on hands and knees in Phu Tho Stadium, assembling
a jigsaw puzzle of 551,232 pieces, 48 x 76, a leisurely pastime

where blood ran in alleys, and tanks fumed on expansive boulevards
and when it was done, a lotus flower appeared, with six petals

symbolic of renewal, optimism and eternal serenity
around the corner, from me, three mother's, used to gather to play mahjong
on Thursday night, when their boys were "overseas"
On Friday Seale laid out an enormous jigsaw puzzle on her dining room table
completed it by Sunday dinner, a different one every month
She would say, "it's what God does with your life, puts it together, then you take
it apart, and spend the rest of your life putting it back together"

One month, that puzzle had a piece she prayed would never show up
But did, David was gone in a firefight in Hue
And she lit a candle for him on the exact day she found out
he had passed away, until she did

yeah, Seale it's a puzzle, that we think we know how to play
turn pieces over and fuse them to bring order to our days
of all the places for the biggest jigsaw puzzle to be assembled
the irony chills us to our bones, that nothing makes any sense
or can be reasoned away

The Ball Drops with No one There

Been alone on New Year's Eve for a half dozen years
cheap champagne in crystal glasses, long legged gals in gowns,
silly hats and glasses, old men dancing with their hands on their
wives asses mixed memories of years passed

full moon casts it shadow
orange flames warm clutches of hardy souls
sitting with Roman candles, made in China, bought in Mexico
waiting to make a show, hoot, but not shoot the shotgun
in the truck

what of me this night after a darkened year
that smells of smoke from fires barely quelled
of politicians preening for attention, protestors
looting and burning for social justice, a virus that
the smart guys with degrees, couldn't send to
hell

In this canvas chair, watching that Times Square ball
Where millions would stand, and blow horns, scream
and kiss whoever as near them at midnight
no noise, streets black and cold, only the damaged
souls left to watch it go

got a dandy 7/11 chicken parm
microwaved it in three minutes
some green tea, and a bowl of pretzels
that moon rises before me
searching for chicken, not much of it
attempting to stay on the moment, making it
seem serene, not wanting any memories backward
its all painful there
no thoughts about what tomorrow may bring
just waiting for that ball to drop and pray
I'm still above ground to say

Happy New Year 2021

Defacing Abe

The great emancipator
freed the slaves
forced amendments through to
protect us all, expanded rights to
former slaves and us all
saved the damn union
offered eloquence when others
spewed venom
had his brains splattered at Ford's theater
shared Rushmore with Washington
never owned a slave
cried for the dead, prayed for peace instead
of war, maintained his humor, even as depression,
personal loss grew, would not be overwhelmed by
grief for he or Martha or the nation
soldiered on, always

who cares
not the bastards who threw red paint on
his statue, in front of the San Francisco City Hall
where Harvey Milk was assassinated
why did they want to cancel Abe
splash him red, the plaque at its base

obliterated by the paint's pooling?

not a black coalition or even Johnny Rebs
but the Sioux contingent to remember
the largest executive ever on one December 26th
in 1862, when 38 warriors were executed after
the brutal uprising in Dakota

Abe review the cases, commuted 265 warriors of
their war crimes, but 38 he could not abide, their
ferocity and unimaginable acts, he could not turn away
so he said ok, to their deaths that day

and on this day after Xmas, when you could not
find five souls who knew or care, a Sioux came forward
to display his angst from 158 years ago
to underscore that the union he saved is not united
anymore, enough identity groups at any moment to claim
reparations, legislation, notice, even fame by
taking down or pissing with paint on at least one man
we should all be able to revere.

All the Guys I Know

With whom I have lost touch mostly
reach out to as years start, for a birthday wish
or more likely when one of us is dead
seem to have a malady that that cheerily
note, they are licking or managing with a
stoic resolve that always is an amazement
not a one whines, or sobs, loses composure
or allows for or wants any pity

how they got it always seems just
serendipitous, the forces just came
special delivery to be unpacked one morning
or afternoon, when the wife was out playing
with her friends at hatha yoga, talking to Sol the
butcher about the prime ribs, or just buying cheap wine
to go with enough pasta and gravy to feed the Navy

Ike tells me:
"I'm recovering from a radical prostatectomy"
"doing fine"
Expects to live long enough he said to start taking his
Viagra again
Panglossian to be sure, but I drop whatever it was I called about

To say I'll pray for him

Jersey Dan is already deep into chemo for bladder cancer
And he writes, "they tell me this is the best cancer to have"
Which I would never expect, but he pees fluorescent colors
Into a bottle by his bed, and finds the drugs send him on trips
like the old days, he laments

Only Cosmo seems to have that inner wisdom
that comes from knowing its over, he only converses in
Kantian tones, and has adopted existentialism as his guide
through, the cancer, he has, revealed now,long hidden
in his pancreas, quickly metastasized
the palliative some morphine by product ended the pain
leaving behind a haze of thoughts only summoned by philosophers
and the walking dead

more gone than here a shrinking
inner circle of decaying men
aware of being in the third act
hoping for a benign ending in a script penned by
someone else
with just a few more pages left
and a desire to not leave the stage too
soon or failing that die
wailing, in pain, and praying finally
for mercy from the forces that have
darkened all of our lives

Her Fingers on His Lips

Twain regaled visitors to
Stormfield, one of his retreats
Roaming in a red robe bestowed
By Oxford swells
Cigars and scotch whiskey sat in
visitor rooms, to melt the consternation of
being in the presence of this master of the story
his presence overwhelming for some

not a girl who was both deaf and blind
who met him, and became friends for life
Twain got her into Radcliffe
So she became the first ever mute to earn a
Bachelors degree

He would sit by the light
His white mane agleam
Open his scarlet robe, with book in one hand
And pipe in the next
And she would sit by his knee
Put her fingers on his lips
As he would read then
motion too quickly to follow

her assistant would grab her hand
on the palm frantically sign to stay with him
and she would run her hand over his full face
and in his hair
and see him there in her mind

Twain knew what she could abide
That thinking is aided by voice and eye
But essence lies deeper inside
And what he was, and could say touched
Every single day they stayed in that august
place, where he read to her into the night
So to Helen Keller is was no small thing
"he treated me like a competent human being
that is why I loved him….There was about him, the
air of one who suffered greatly"
something she knew about, but did not focus upon
nor did he, even when Twain brought others to his humor
he rarely smiled
Keller observed, he smiled not with his mouth
But with his mind, and when he wanted to reach her mind he took her fingers
to his lips, spoke softly, and slow, so she could get every word.

Intersectional Literature

Can you hear the banging of pots and pans
the discordant sounds, of haters, hackers, self
anointed and appointed censures of what you say and
read
the un- medicated defilers of what they do not want you
to read, bookshelf cleaners, knuckle dragging purveyors of
the acceptable and the normative for a culture stripped
of its culture, plucked clean of the feathers to fly, gutted
by identity groupers who only know what is today, crush
all yesterdays, cry out to not be victimized, but use it as the core
of their identity
universal haters of all that is before, no bonfire needed,
electrons eradicated, Big Tech taking up the theme, shut down
everyone else's volume, paper, and dream
no matches needed, no stakes to erect, no faggots to collect
and still you can get, off, on hearing old men scream

better be in the present day vernacular
F Scott Fitzgerald, poor old Dr. Seus
Padma Venkatraman, a young force of today's lit
screams,
'if it comes from a time of racism, sexism, homophobia,
ableism, whatever that is, and white supremacy" it just shouldn't be read

anymore, anywhere
is it about misogyny, does a woman get shamed, is violence the theme
do the identity folks succeed or are they all defamed
a cacophony of slurs, about Homer, Twain, and Hawthorne
forget about Hemingway who checks all the boxes in this
intersectional hall of fame or shame

On the way to taking it all away
Classics thrown into the dumpster of the discarded
All headed for the landfill of words of meaning decomposing
For the lit of anger, ignorance, eternal despair, bringing on
a generation of the here and now, who can barely read anything
past 140 words, a culture of mutterers, humming tunes about penises,
un-manicured body parts, and a revolution of the intellectually disabled
unable to elevate themselves out of a bed in mom's house
or take their eyes off their phone long enough to see
anything, let alone read, Homer, who?

Tranquility Lost

It's been a too long week
dog's bark in the halls
their owners do not care
chins down, eyes buried in some screen
texting nothing back and forth
caught in a twisted Freudian dream

So you get your shorts on, tie your shoes
for that run on the hard sand, as the sun
turns the bay, that orange color that soothes
and you expect everyone else will be in some
state of chill, arm in arm, sitting by a fire,
watching the day go, Sunday dissolving with the
sun into quiet darkness

but not a chance
the rich boys have tied five boats and a yacht
together, anchored and playing with
8 foot speakers, some rap song that has the same
beat and lyric, endlessly
the DJ abroad, inserts his claim, what a night
to Par- teee

the girls dance with midriffs bare, shaking long
multi- colored hair, the narcissists drink, Tequila
and Johnny Walker, Red
have nothing else in mind, not a care for another
mom and pop, on a couch in La Jolla, watching 60 minutes
lamenting the end of the Republic, as their progeny blasts
noise over, an otherwise tranquil bay
loosing their worries and minds, and place in this time
to liquor and women, in a sunset trance

curse them for the freedom wealth allows
the rest of us,wondering about next month's rent
only wanted a respite from all that
only to find five boats, full of the entitled
laughing, drinking, and shaking their tight asses

tranquility comes not from what you hear and see
unfortunately, it ensures only and always from
within

Shift the Damn Gestalt

Whenever government came to be it was to organize
to put someone or body in charge of delivering
basic things to the folks around the glen, in the valley
or down a rutted road

Divine rights Kings, sultans, oligarchs, dictators, emancipators,
corrupt collaborators, narcissistic bloviators, even a few men of the people
all had the similar focus
maintain power, war if you must, conquer and turn to dust all in the way of
whatever, it is that maintains the body politic
care for the upper echelon, collect taxes, fill your coffers first and often
let the others scramble, but not too much to revolt, for food, shelter,
and a degree or happiness, providing security along the way

even so, government was in the background mostly through the ages
until you had a say, every few years, of who would stay or go
the gestalt was clear, government in the background, your life upfront
a comfortable figure/ground array, Kurt Koffka would say, as
would his colleagues Max and Wolfgang who proclaimed when what is
background moves forward, just watch out

Leviathon of debt, strangle hold on our earnings, director of our
attitudes, enforcer of what we say, whom we embrace, and erase

shoved into our faces, what we once ignored, required to pay attention
even if we are just plain bored, or afraid to say
the stench of it is in our nostrils, a virus of control, sickening a nation
that just wants to be left alone

it needs to travel back in space, shift the damn Gestalt
give us back our freedoms, solitude, let us find our own way
protect from danger here and there, have enough nukes to blow the
world away 80 times
put the taxes I send you to good use
care for those who can't quite make it on their own
be about the future, where what kills us is gone, except
for what we bring on ourselves
end the prohibitions, be about what is now and next
bury the issues of the past, and get on with it

change the damn Gestalt, put everything back in place
let our lives dominate, and make all believe that
once again it is about
We the People

The Facel Vega Hits a Tree

Confirming life's absurdity
The existentialists always claimed that's the
way things are, all those precious plans,
preparations contortions to get what you desire
is useless mostly, any day or time, until the end
catches up to you and you are freed from your
ennui and total despair

The French could not agree, on context or that reality
Sartre fought Camus
Jabbed each other incessantly
Until that gorgeous Facel Vega HK 500 hit a tree
With Camus in a luxurious bucket seat riding
Shotgun
As publisher Michel Gallimard drove
His wife and daughter in the backseat
Sheltered from the crash
Camus dies without a word
Michel with only a few days to reflect
Before he also is in the past

Absurd enough Sartre would reflect
Even if others still suspect

That Soviet bad guy, Dmitri Shepilov
Set it up out of hatred for Albert who
called him out for that massacre of Hungarians
In 1956

Or was it more the support Camus
threw at Boris Pasternak of Dr. Zhivago fame
who embarrassed the Kremlin with a Noble Prize
so red faced, they made him turn it down
Shepilov had much to bear due the loud mouth
And pen of this French existentialist who knew
No matter how uncertain, and unplanned, life
Still required integrity and truth to be a justified
man
no matter how great the thinking
contribution, or adulation, the "unbearable
absurdity "levels us all to the same result
say what you must
never retreat from what matters to you
expect nothing, know your plans will likely
be dashed, and how you planned to go after
a long life lived is always an
absurdity

The Jockey and the Showgirl

5' 8" in flats, Marlene,
in her heels 4 more inches taller than that
Rockette legs, 34's, long swan neck
skin without pores, soft movie star voice
more Garbo than Bacall
when she walked into the clubhouse
silence came
the hucksters and gamers, paused between
parleys to watch her walk to his table

there at 5'4 "Sammie sat, slick black hair
open shirt and a 18 karat smile, put his left hand on her
neck, showing off his diamond rings, pulled her towards
his lips
the jockey with the most wins, that year, flew her in
from Vegas, just to hand around for the meet
and when it was over, just repeat the cycle
of high times, hard liquor, and a women so out of his
league, it seemed, to everyone but him

Sammie served as best man at wedding one
Only a few years out of high school
he loved horses, but loved attention too

was a world class gymnast and martial artist, piled up
ribbons, and hardware trophies,
he saved my ass a few times from a beating by the local
toughs
when summer winds blew across the school yard, we'd pile into his
GTO and head for the shore, before casinos, big hotels, and high priced
broads, just beach and ocean and an old boardwalk to sleep under
at night

it was 60 miles that he did in 45 minutes
he had wood blocks on the gas pedal and the brake
so he could stand and race towards the destination
before radar detectors, car phones, and troopers out
to get you

no one had more discipline
to always make the weight in his riding days
I saw him eat just three peanuts on flight to LA
Broke them in half for lunch
And one night, he revealed how he would
feel satiated, eating a half gallon of vanilla ice cream
and then flip it, vomiting into the hotel room's
toilet bowl

50 years evaporate, he stayed with her all the way
married a month after me, but he figured out how to stay
bonded, always seeing her as she was, and she saw him the same way
in their minds they were ageless
the forces still come, no matter what you will for them to stay away
her memory faded, he put her away, pretended she recognized

him on visitors day
dark clouds turned black, a bad cough and fever came
and in a moment, she placed her last bet
Sammie called me, talked about her as if it was
all those years ago, he only saw the long legged,
showgirl, that took his breath away,
a thoroughbred, he said, and she was all those years
and to her dying,last day.

Where did all the Vices Go?

Never had them, in play
the vices of my day
Cardinal Spellman would come on
Sunday and say, your soul is at grave risk
If you dare embrace
Envy, gluttony, greed,
lust, that constant standby,catchall
sloth
and throw in arrogance to parents, priests,
teachers and your sister
and the vice of young men
anger, resentment and revenge that
it can bring
all of the above vices of consequence
that damage you within
even if, they are not
mortal sins

grave they are not necessarily
I never felt separated from God's grace
felt let out, when the toughs from Father Judge
went through their litany of what was
venial and what was not

pretending that the penance they were assigned
for beating kids at school, stealing, lunches,
and screwing their girlfriends in the back seat
of a Buick, were nothing more than youthful
explorations, nothing grave at all
a few hail Mary's would redeem them all

Chased girls, collected glossy magazines,
envied for a very short while, the guys who scored fast
cars, long legged women, and always had cash
never had the time
for sloth, food never turned me on,
lusted after many, most remained a muse
thought beer and booze, a waste of money,
denying reality came naturally, liquor was never needed
lied too much, to just get by
walked crooked paths

at 11, in the breezeway of Spruance Elementary
right under the name of the Admiral who won at
Midway and the Philippine Sea, after getting the command
when Halsey had shingles, and sent him instead
who was so cool under fire, they called him
"electric brain"
and had no vices, except he made hot chocolate everyday
and smoked his pipe, as he tended his post war garden

a pack of Camel's was displayed
and the gang was learning how to inhale
which I could not do, and did not want to

never put a reefer, toke,or Marlboro in my lips
and was laughed at and ostracized

all those vices, never adopted or enjoyed
and those that I did have faded
everyone adopted by a friend came to kill
them in the end
smoking, booze and red meat, obesity, envy
and that anger at the world for all they thought it
did to them
a life within the lines, no vices to define you,
and what, on balance, does it get you, the straight and
the narrow
another day above ground, to do something with
the life still within you.

Hang Mike Pence

"Hang Mike Pence! Hang Mike Pence"
the mob screamed, armed and shielded
men and some women, with guns, spears,
and pipe bombs

vandals at the steps of the Capitol
the Visigoths, taking Rome, the Romans
sacking Carthage, Jacobins at the Bastille,
the hungry at the Tzars palace
all with unfulfilled claims of injustice and
all to blame, but themselves
intent upon bringing a living hell into
congressional chambers

no great causes here
zealots of causes imagined and unclear
jumbled prejudice and fear, as old as
modern man
Qs who believe a cabal of pedophiles are running
things, directed by Jews, of course
men with shirts that say "Camp Auschwitz"
others with 6 MINE
six million is not enough

and the companions of the KKK
Proud Boys who play with napalm and pipe bombs
cowards that mobs embolden

men in animal skins, Mad Max faces
prepped by a tortured President to
frighten, destroy, and hold a nation hostage
on a January day when the election to be
approved, and his loss obvious, to everyone
but these bastards, with the mobs only
precept
"might makes right"
The cops retreated, the proceedings stopped cold
Chanting for Mike Pence to be hung in a gallows
they constructed nearby, because he refused to say
let's come back another day

more mob than cops
the authorities brought the cavalry too late
allowing them to defile
whatever they chose to break, toss,
and spit on
by 2:30 a cop kills a woman crawling through
a window
a cop is crushed to death
five die in all

that mystic chord of memory
Lincoln opined was part of us for all time
Across battle fields to patriot graves

Silenced this day, only a discordant wail
of pain and sorrow now that any of
this happened on this day

they could not find Pence to hang him
but would have certainly if they could
democracy went on that night as the vote turned
the sitting bully into another footnote
where hours before the mob roared
obscenities, left, basically unscathed to fight
another day

and the noose waved in the wind
Pence straightened his tie, pulled his hand
over his hair, and gaveled the session done

and we all pretended it was a nightmare
that would leave us at dawn
and scared as hell that it would not

Sweet N' Low

The EMT got there as soon as they could
Less than three minutes from the firehouse to
620 Park Ave
No need for Manny and Dominic to run up flights of
stairs, or carry the defibrillator on their backs

that man they came upon was gone
his skull obliterated by the fall from the
million dollar apartment on the 11th floor
arms and legs askew, broken too
and his blood already running towards the sewers

the doorman knew the who
told the ME guys as they carefully reassembled his
old man's frame into a body bag
"It's Mr. Tober ... It's Tober for sure
11th floor"

And so it was that Donald Tober
Made his fortune focused on everything
you put around your cup of coffee,
first sugar in little packets, then non –
dairy creamer, more raw sugar combination

until they took artificial sweeteners put
into a cute pink package and named
it Sweet N' Low

in no time Tober had it in 80% of everyplace you
go to have coffee, and then everything else
he sweetened the world,
artificially
and gave back mightily for his good fortunes
grateful for his Harvard degree, his savvy,
instincts, and a life companion who always
encouraged his sense of gratefulness for what they
had

by 89, the forces got him
always do, everyone gets the same bullet
no one knows just when it is ever do
his hollow point came as Parkinson's
that one night, he could no longer
abide

what is a life without some sweetness in each day
that has to be authentic and not
artificial in anyway
imaginations, illusions from drugs and the
disease
muscular spasms, uncontrolled or not
destroying a lifestyle cherished and by
memory, still cogent, unforgotten

who can know the final thoughts of
any man, before he ends it all
what flashes vividly, what is finally forgotten
and then the leap of faith that the next
move will end it all
and open that unopened door to the
unknown, where pain, and torment are not
admitted, and you return to your essence
eternally
or so we hope
opening that Sweet N' Low just won't be
as mindless anymore
at least for a while

They're Dying in the ICU's

With no one around to kiss them goodbye
Tubed up, to breathing machines
pushing, O2 in and out, past virus attacked
lungs, unable to sustain a breath, without
pain
lost souls, not seeing the dawn bend toward them
or aware of the sunsets, just down the way
where their sons and daughters stay
hoping for a salvation call that
does not come

the dying old
entrapped by a spiked protein
strangling, intubated, sedated
last face seen before they pass
soft eyes, encased my a plastic shield
a pale blue mask, still yearning for it all to
pass, and rarely does

thoughts, as I wait
in my car alone, in the rain
with a few hundred others to get
the "shot" to save us from an intubated

sedated demise
wonder what is on their minds
how to pay the rent, get enough food,
get their grandkids back to school,
the insanity of having "shots" and not enough
getting them into arms
giving them to marijuana dispensary workers
and holding teachers back
why anyone would say no, out of fear
or more likely stupidity engendered by the
senseless, dumb and useless, of the internet
mob

patience required here as the minutes go
all of us on the perimeter of the Forum
where Kareem played
now a place as over its prime as all of us
in our cars

the hourly folks under garbage bags, helping
attempting cheerfulness as they take your
temperature
"98.4, sir, not bad"
Grab your license
"hey, you look a lot younger in person"
And inject you
"nothing to worry about here"
And get a fist bump from her lavender gloved
Hand
All the eyes over the masks

Say the same
"I know this sucks, but, it will be over soon"
And
You go along
Shelve your ongoing societal critique
Consternation about who is calling the shots
Disdain for all politicians, ruling elites,
Everyone who just knows, all of us in our cars
Are below them, chumps
I turn to the last classic music station
I can find
And its Bela Bartok, Romanian dances, for Christ sake
esoteric, and unknown
just like my deltoid
draped out the window
awaiting some hope from the contents
of a syringe

Nobody Cares What I Think

When you're a player in your forties
Apex of your prime
You let go of your inhibitions, about everything
Screw without remorse, align with no moral course
spout theories, designs, notions, and outrageous demands
on everyone under your control
you play the role, it becomes you
ego driven, hormonally released, unrepentant
master of the universe

Convinced it is not hubris
only passion, wit, intelligence
and guile
an audience of long legged admirers
sharp upwardly mobile lieutenants
and grisly old men, vicariously enjoying
your success

then the forces come
the universe shrinks
the grandiose yields to mundane
at dawn, the old leaps and bounds

are replaced by the inner dialogue
of just getting one leg out bed
before sunrise

rockstar crowds, evaporated
a conference room of tepid coffee drinkers
more concerned about the delivery on their
sushi lunch than that long imagined plan
in your overdone powerpoint

you actually have more to say
deep inner meanings, you get Marcus
Aurelius, understand K shaped recovery curves,
Want to explore graphite water filtration, quantum computing,
And sexual robots driven by AI
No one is listening to:

What you believe the 14th amendment is for, why Title IX needs review, the role of anti – trust in turning Google into digital dust, how keto diets are a dangerous ruse, electric cars a scam, our lack of rare earth chemicals a strategic flaw, why the Gerald Ford 13. 2 billion aircraft carrier is a disaster, why relationships are out of touch with morality, what happens when Islam is the world's dominant faith, and why is it more of us are losing faith, in everything

still you go on
trying not to be a drain or challenge
just to get through a day

quietly playing at expanding what you know
without telling anyone so
afraid to annoy with an original thought
hoping to get your must have list
reduced to its obvious absurdity

enough money to shelter, eat, and buy
meds and gas
and healthy enough to be present
enough to enjoy it
mastering that is enough
more than enough

Would They Banish Christ on Twitter

Jesus was not a rock star in his time
Andrew Lloyd Weber aside
Gospel hype came later
Rome ruled and murdered until the
Emperor's joined up out of real politic
Leaving faith and supplication for another time

Christ was outcast, lunatic, another prophet of
The God of Abraham, who the priests deplored
Population mostly ignored, and Rome crucified
To restore the order they cherished more than
Anything, and to cover their lush butts, from the
Domos back in Rome, who just wanted their lucre
And nothing much else

Even old Fyodor took a pause with his brothers
Karamazov, as Ivan tells the Tale of the Grand Inquisitor
Winds up in a cell with the Savior himself, in Seville,
And attempts to convince to not come back as the
Messiah right now, it would kill the Church you see
That has grown past what Christ offered on the mound
Oh, says the Inquisitor, "man can live by bread alone"
And does not need God, when his mind is controlled, and creature

Comforts are assured, freedom matters less, men want control
A well worn path, not transcendence at all"
Christ listens, does not speak
Kisses the Grand Inquisitor on his "bloodless, aged lips"
And is released, not burned at the stake, does not return
As Messiah to upset the apple carts of history
Ivan finishes
content he has proven is utter distaste for all religion

Is Ivan, Jack Dorsey
With Rasputin beard, and a forum called twitter
Who denies people access, if they are "civically" irresponsible
Would Jesus be there @therealCHrist
Or would be electronically crucified for his views
Of the time on Twitter 30 AD

I believe in one God
I am the son of God
Whoever believes in me will not perish…but
Have everlasting life

Against the Roman zeitgeist
of a pantheon of Gods
A Hebrew God who now has a son
Born of a virgin Jewess
Who turns the other cheek, but
Challenges the priests and Rome at the same time
Who want this heretic, and radical on their platform
So he can recruit more Jews, to be a Jew like him?

Could Dorsey resist the pressure to remove this
Civically unfit, radical, proselytizing Jew?
Or would he banished for life too

Then in other years what would he do
With Galileo, Copernicus, Da Vinci, Buddha,
Confucius, Columbus, Picasso, and maybe even
Einstein

Ban them all for being outside the mainstream
Ideas that might actually change the direction
Force a new selection, demand recollection and
Encourage disaffection from what is now and before
A worn path of yesterday, afraid of that trail to the
Unknown

Christ would be eliminated, and the Romans untouched

Worn Out from the Inside Out

The bearings are shot inside
Big Jimmy would say after a
long day, plugging holes in tires gone bad
unloading the new ones, re- treading a pile
one story high for resale, to kids with GTO's
and their father's Fords

Light a Dutch Master, hold it in
greased fingers and sigh to me
leaning on the outside wall of
my Uncle Harry's Tire Store
"I'm 33 kid, worn out, from the
Inside out"
But he always came back, didn't miss a
day for, not one, for the next twenty years
without a complaint or whine, just a good man
always there to do his job, and always on time

was it stamina
resolve, upbringing?
no other place to go
enough to show, and carry on
feed the three boys, house Melinda

care for his Pops and Grandma, and hers as
too, until they all went underground, which he paid for
as well

few diversions, no broads on the side
cigars, a shot of Walker now and then, a single Malt
for big occasions, lifted weights in the garage
played pick up basketball at the downtown Y
coached football with Pop Warner little guys
had no other obvious destination but getting
by, and exhibited every trait, one would consider
of a good guy

Yet, I whine when the rains come, when the full moon
is shrouded by thick clouds, as cash is gone in days,
for the cleaners, gas, and rent to pay
every day brings repetition, deja' vu between actions,
the twinkle and charm faded, a lack of relevance signals
existential alarm
I'd rather light a big cheap cigar
lean against a sharp car, smell of grease and oil
smile at a kid and say, "I'm worn out from the inside out, but I wouldn't have it
any other way"

Just Leave Me the hell alone

I've listened to the sax player wail
"Summertime when the living is easy…"
Under the bridge by the Central Park zoo
Heard, homeless, opera man sing arias, holding out a cup
By Carnegie hall
Took in Shakespeare in the Park, that
Joe Papp started
Watched women dance in East side studios
As I ate a soft pretzel on the street
Imaging what I should not have with any of them
In their leotards and unwrapped hair

All had discreet talents
even the old man in the purple beret
painting a common bridge, in the open air, like he
was Monet, on a spring day, he saw a beautiful
spring, that only he could see, in oil on canvas
now- indelibly

I have no such talent, visible or ethereal on which to
Cling
If everything stops, with an X- ray, a colonoscopy,
A blood test of some sort, a finger up my ass, revealing

A swollen something that must be eradicated, irradiated,
Reduced or removed by a scalpel at the end of a surgeons'
Hand or a robots

I have no grand talent of which the world would be deprived

Cut me so
I can melt into a soiled old chair
Watch the NBA, smile at a young man's touchdown
Change my dripping bandages, clean out the Hickman in
My chest
Empty the bottle at my feet, oil the catheter
Flush the contents of the colostomy bag,
Rip off some tape across the hair on my nipples
So I can have a night of nightmares
Awaken at 3 am, and not know where the hell I am

For what, a few more years, rather than go now
When I see a face and cannot recall a name at all
Lee Marvin, Robert Vaughn, Robert Wagner, Natalee Wood,
James Coburn, Audie Murphy, all come after contemplation
Even old friends that are still above ground, I nod at and hug
And it takes through lunch to realize who I am with
Maybe the Doc should save that scalpel for another dude
Who has some talent left to cultivate, who could handle a few more rounds
I'm shadowboxing now, punching at the shadows of my life
And its all shadows on walls
With no horn to blow, song to sing,
Palette of oils to brush with a brash abandon

On the canvas of my life once an impasto
Landscape of depth and color, now faded
Watercolors

Hey, Doc
Just leave me the hell alone
I'm a humming closed engine, like an ole' Rolls
Let it fade on its own
Go cut someone else
Who still has something to give....

Mortified

I wish I was dead
No really, I do
Forgetting tings I should know
Consciousness directed elsewhere
To supposed significant and weighty
Concerns of the society at large
Pretending that by conjuring about it all
Gravitas comes, to a life, already past
Its prime, straining for relevance
A knowing nod to delay the passing of
Time

So self –involved and centered on
The individuation of who I am
Losing in that existential quest my
Real place and impact on
The now, not then, next or
May be

There are excuses, dead branches on
A dying tree
Monster gut pain, enemy of sleep
Eating at bananas, white rice, applesauce

From baby jars, and burnt toast
only
for the last six days
hiding the malady from others view
exploding in bathrooms from here to there
living between spasms

bad back from lifting weights
young man squats on old man's
knees
lower lumbar, level 6 pain
and that familiar incisor shouting
"fix me" for the last five years

Excuses, ego, existential exhaustion
Not enough to explain away
Why
I forgot my 32 year old daughters'
Birthday today
She sent me a straightforward text
"I'm 32 Dad, remember?
My birthday was three days ago"
So I called mortified, stammered
Through the standard I'm sorry, and it's
Not about anything, except, I forgot
Getting old, and spouted out the litany
Often offered for sorrow and grief

She was generous and bemused
But certainly confused, and anger

Was there too, even if hidden
Unconvinced
It was not because I loved her less
Or was lazy to say, "I love you"
I was just too self- centered and inner
Directed to realize that she mattered
And needed me- it never came to mind
And is that a seminal crime, a felony of the heart
Punishable by exile, the cold shoulder, and
Never breathing again?

Mortified again….

The Rape of Xinjiang

Rape the weapon of choice for
conquerors, oppressive regimes hands
Ultimate power play of might over
Decency
Degradation, shame, pure evil
Penetrating body and soul
Depravity
Victors go unpunished as women's
Bodies broken

No time is free of it
The bell tolls for them
Sabine women
The rape of Nanking
SS rapes in the camps
1.4 million raped by Soviets overtaking German towns
Yezidi's raped by the Islamic State

Always during and after war
Now a tool to sustain control of
ethnic minorities, signal an end to
freedom and a death knell to liberty
systemic, ingrained, as the salute or firing

an AK-47
ask
Turnay Ziawudin, a Turkic ethnic
Uighur from Xianjiang, 1 million
are imprisoned there by the will of
Xi Jinping, the supposed modern leader
Bent on making China the predominant power
and pervasive place

one hundred women watch a girl be stripped
and confess to crimes against the state
then she is gang raped
Turnay turns away, for that?

An electric prod penetrates her vagina
Anus penetrated with a stick
Days later gang raped as well

This same story thousands of women can
Tell- to someone
If anyone is listening to the testimony
Xi knows the world will turn its back
Some chatter of stopping it
He knows there will be no retribution
Saying
"they are all actors disseminating false information"

Nothing fake here
Systemic rape Chinas sharp knife
Cutting the heart out of ethnic Muslims

Because they just want to be left alone and
Follow their own path

All the "influencers" are too self involved to
see or care, new Presidents sympathize
pontificate, puff and well up in tears,
words go around the world from the East River
to the Hague
nothing
as the Chinese troops drop their pants
and obey orders, as screams overtake the
call to prayer in Urumqi
and a people tremble, as they suck on tender duck
in Beijing

On Any Given Super Bowl Sunday

All the streets are clear
a nation pauses, takes a sabbatical
for a few hours as uniquely talented men
play a complex game with goals in sight
and mind, and the rest of inside watching
as though it was our boys, sons, and brothers
locked in the combat of the gridiron
on this Sunday
I watch it too, now, alone
no chips and brew, attempting to get the
antenna tuned, so I can watch the old man throw
and the young QB shuttle, but fail at it mostly
until I find the Spanish station that's carrying it
live, don't need the damn narration, easy enough
to figure whose ahead and behind, and if the bookies
will lose on the spread

wander over the PBS, when the signal goes sideways
and find Bizet, from the Met
Carmen the Gypsy seductress luring poor
Don Jose 'away from his girlfriend, his life,
And his sanity, with her jacked up skirts,
Bosom, and voice of guts and sultry timbre

Watch it on and off until ACT ll, when the toreador
Enters, and the stage fills with his famous song

Outside the window, a cycle skids after crossing a
double yellow into a tall woman's old Buick, he's flat in
his back, the cycle on its side
the woman screams, then dials
Engine 21 shows up, leaving the game for this
They stabilize his neck,leave his helmet on
And splint his legs, which are broken but not
Gone
The old QB throws more winners, its almost a runaway
At the half, the EMT's get the guy on a stretcher
And the cops open up a path
She grabs cop for stability and sobs into his ear
And he holds her for a moment, until the
panic passes

I do what I always do at the half for the last 25 years
Run until the half time show passes
Jog by the bars, and parties, watch the guys
Eye their dates, pitcher empty, then filled again
No one seems to care who the hell is performing
For seven million dollars on the fifty yard line
Why bother you wonder
When I eye that's its over, I increase my cadence
Some, and get back just as the kick- off has come

Carmen has rejected Don Jose
Who cannot stand, she has given him up for
The handsome bullfighter…
More scores by the G.O.A.T.
A drama almost over
Triumph awaits the victor

Don Jose threatens with his blade
Carmen cries, 'Kill me, or let me go"
He cries, with the angst of a man who so wanted
Something, he could never have, and was to blinded
To have any clarity, that he was doomed

The final seconds pass
The Bucs win, Brady seems invincible at 43
They hug family and each other
300 million cheer, and clean up the living rooms

Don Jose' stabs her, holds her
As she bleeds out, and is
Taken away
And I am in tears not for the victory
At Tampa Bay, but the sweet, heart break
of a man who gave up everything for a
woman, who never loved him
and both payed the price on this
Superbowl Sunday

And the traffic resumed
McDonald's sold more burgers
The pizza joints scraped up the fallen dough
The drunks fell asleep on Uncle Morty's couch
and nobody wanted to go home and face
Monday, with nothing to look forward to until
The NCAA.

That Vacuum Cleaner

Who knows what changes your life
or just a day
most think it's the existential stuff
dreams, self- expression, releasing the Giant Within
crap
listening to the inner voice
shutting up and saying less
cultivating silence
reaching for that internal "knowing"
getting unattached, being detached
not giving a good God damn
finding God, rejecting God
being spiritual instead
enjoying the now, and sustaining the presence in
the present

all of that, surely, helps
get you out of a rut that is cavernous
extricate you from the suck up, you've become
reassert your masculinity and purpose
just to become again whatever the hell you
were before life knocked you on your ass

yet, the things have set me free are not
ethereal at all, mundane, utilitarian
in design
a wipe with Mr. Clean that whitens toilet
bowls and tubs
large garbage bags that hold a week of refuse
a razor that does not irritate
two towels that keep my bones dry after a shower
and this

Bissell vacuum, my word
Its sucks up a year of imbedded carpet schmutz
Has a pleasant motor sound, just loud enough to
Annoy the neighbors up and down, whose mutts
spoil any afternoon nap
and is just plain fun to pull around
what was once a unseemly space is now
a habitable place

You can have your séances, and retreats, your
Jungian, Freudian, and CBT therapists
Give me a vacuum, to suck away my troubles, anytime

Exiled

Wind cuts through you
ceaselessly on this ancient, dormant,
volcanic mound
trees in forest when Darwin ambled the
up and down terrain, no flat stretch
anywhere

1200 miles off an Africa shore
South enough to be near nothing and
No one
Where Bonaparte ended
on a coach, under a canopy
without fanfare, a last breath of a fallen
Emperor, uncrowned
exiled but not forgotten

he had a grand vision
that wanted more than the ancien' regime
could abide
took noble ideas to their extreme
hoped to spread liberte', egalite', fraternite'
at first, but became entranced by power
over compensation, delusions of grandeur, and narcissism

that was just obscene
republic to empire, empire to overextension, excesses,
and a world fed up, with his codes, and wanting to return to
the status quo
antebellum

no impeachments
no show trials
no summary execution
not like Khadaffi, or Saddam
no special units to blast you away at some
mountain hideaway, a la, Osama

exile was the way
unfortunately not available for misdeeds today
to Elba for nine months
only to stage an masterful escape
return to accolades for 100 days
until Wellington assembled at Waterloo
and ended it for Bonaparte finally too

there are always Waterloo's
whether Appomatix, Tet, or Hiroshima
emperors fade, fall, and die, buried in
elaborate places, their movements with them
and whatever good they may have done
forgotten, as Anthony claimed for Caesar

would the modern world be better off if
exile still remained, where a damned leader could still

take a freighter or the RMS St. Helena to this worn
rock pile, south of everywhere
to live out what's left, with no place to play 18 holes,
drink a Diet Coke, grab a Bud, or, even watch the world
you wanted to run go on without you, on a wide screen
tv

and dream of a comeback, like Bonaparte
from Elba, if only for a mere 100 days just
to prove to yourself, they still love you
and then return to lie on an old bed, with
only the memories of grandeur to keep you
up at night.

Now Pauly is Gone

Augie sent an email
nobody calls anymore
Pauly is gone is all it said
I slumped down even further into my
only chair
and brought up an image in my mind's eye
usually for me, frozen at 16,
sitting on a stoop in the old neighborhood
telling filthy jokes, claiming to getting laid,
and getting paid by old man Stein, the butcher
for delivering before Sabbath

Pauly lived in the next rowhouse
we didn't share a concrete step
shared everything else
his older brother Ron's having his mother's approval
a distant father, like most of us had, his surviving
Guadacanal
His taking any job, now that he had "working papers"
so he could afford to take his dates to the movie
on Castor Avenue

he was handsome, had long curly hair, a clear skin

no acne at all, big grey eyes, and generally looked like
James Dean, who we all idolized, as a throwback, our
counterpoint and disgust with the
English wave, and even Elvis

Ron got him rubbers from Ponzi's
where we played pinball, Zeke sold
Trojans under the table for a hefty mark up
Pauly actually used his, I had mine in my wallet
for at least a full year

When the toughs from Father Judge crossed
the FDR boulevard to beat up Jews
he stood by me, when we were cornered or
took a chance on our luck and fought back
and left them and us black and blue

mostly, though, I reflected on sitting in his mother's
dining room, playing poker, mostly draw
for nickel, dimes, and quarters, with no double
raise, after school two days a week
when she was working days
lost mostly, but played, between street ball
and the varsity, until my mother called
as did all my guys, and we'd take our cash
and run to smoldering brisquet, or chicken and
chicken soup

who thinks you'll die back then
when there are only horizons to see

and the clouds of life fade every morning
and one warm, gentle friend,like Pauly
makes you hope it all never ends
and then it does as though
there was not a day in between
from what was to now
a life consumed in the interval
between striking a match on the concrete step
and that cigarette always hanging out of his mouth….

No Valentine to Open

On gas station corners
From Bed Sty to Florence and Normandy
folks are selling roses, red vases, and
blown up hearts
a 24 hour gig to entice the unprepared to
bring a Valentine to bear, on someone loved
or loving, where no relationship can't at
least be repaired for one February day

who started it, this scam to be in love
cough off some cash to show you care
or want entry to some sacred, locked up place
that a box of chocolates, a card or two, some
special booze, and throw in a negligee, in case your
intentions might be mistaken

too many damn theories how it all began
a pagan thing, celebrating mother wolves of
the wayward boys, Romulus and Remus
a few imprisoned then executed noblemen
writing last words to some far off spouse
even Chaucer weighed in pretending to know
Never met any dame or male in pursuit of

A kiss and hug, just to hear her say
"I love" … "you" too
Who cared about the derivation or gave it any
Contemplation
Enough to have someone near, you can send and give
Something to, and have an envelope to open

It is a societal expectation
From kindergarten on, pasting, cutting out
Hearts and pasting them to colored paper
A match for every guy, and gal, part of the
Seeking of life's holy grail
Happiness
It seems is a card, candy, and a dozen roses

Never to end
Marriages last forever
Always somebody,somewhere
So goes the mythology, cupid has arrows
For all mortal souls

Then the quiver is empty
The mailbox a dark hole
You have to buy Ms. Foo's flowers for you
And get a heart of Whitman's at the drugstore
Imagine they came from some hot brunette
Walk the dawn alone, let the sun set unseen
Drown out memories with Metallica

Avoid any dream, stay up until it passes
And you haven't slit your wrists and bled out
Roman style in a warm bath

How bad is it anyway, after all these years
To have nothing to open on Valentines Day
And not even shed a tear

Stabbed Twenty Three times on a Mild March Day

Toynbee and Gibbon say all civilizations rise
And fall someday
Historians contend that leaders arise to fit the
circumstances of the day
Where are De Gaul, FDR, Churchill today?

14 February 44 BC
Caesar was given the dictatorship of Rome
for perpetuity
lasted just 30 days, until Brutus and Cassius
huddled with 60 others to end his reign on the spot
and left bleeding from 23 holes, in a body that
was the glory and decadence of Rome

As tall as his soldiers, at 5' 7"
handsome, even as his hairline receded
he exceeded at excess cheating on all three wives
spending 14 years bedding Cleopatra
screwing whoever he could find, dubbed
"the bald adventurer"
Even as his enemies opined
"he was the Queen of Bithynia" for

those early trysts with King Nicomedes
gossips and opponents raised it frequently
how they said he lost his virginity

he was of his times, an adulterer, a covetous snake,
who killed all who defied him in his wake
spent ten years in Gaul, came across the Rubicon in defiance of
the elites, took on Pompey, who took Armenia, Syria, and Palestine
besides ending Spartacus' uprising, nailing him to a cross along
the Apian Way

Pompey was no match for Caesar in his prime
Fighting off Pompey 's larger force at Pharsalus
Forcing the General to flee to Egyptian shores
Where in 48 B.C., his old friend King Ptolemy had
him killed

a leader who had it all
brilliance, bravado, beauty
and claimed it was for Rome
he convinced everyone but the elites who feared
him enough to stab him to death

and it would take Shakespeare to write the play
and put into Anthony's mouth the
eulogy, we all recall from junior high
"I come to bury Caesar, not to praise him,
The evil that men do lives after them, the
Good is oft interred with their bones..
He was my friend faithful and just to me."

And when he was gone
Anthony bedded Cleopatra
Rome ruled for 400 years
And nobody wanted to face
What had happened there and then
"when all men have lost their reason"

No Shakespeare needed to write
The eulogies ahead, if you can find
A leader worthy of it
Where you heart might be in that coffin
No danger of that so far as I can see

Can Hack the Day but not the Night

All writing is therapy
To delay the facing of what is
wrapping yourself in a narrative
confronting that pure white page
Hemingway's, "white bull"
Always getting gored as intensity fades
And fatigue gets onto a page
thoughts to a roads end
falling asleep at the wheel of creation

write, boil water, drink the green ten
pace, shadowbox, scream at the neighbor's dog
"shut up you, f…ing dog"
Write another page, scan the endless useless
correspondence called e- mails
turn everything off until the chapter ends

lay your head on a pillow for ten breaths
awaken two hours later, behind, with napmares
in your head, so real you are afraid to get the mail
which is never of consequence, rejections come quicker now
in texts, everyone displaying an approach- avoidance
syndrome

detached rejections, no file to keep, to throw in anger
across the bedroom floor, or burn behind the apartment
house, at midnight

the day goes by
writing, running, cursing, napping
ranting, writing again
until nothing comes out, grunts subside
as darkness overtakes everything

mood changes as quiet ensues
alone again, just that familiar couple of you
and you
bad company on certain nights
when memory brings the hers back
and that softness is palpable, the smell
on a neck pungent, warmth remembered

and no key you hit, overcomes it
no clever phrase conquers it
this utter, complete, isolation
from anyone and anything that ever really
mattered…

Zephyr in the Kitchen

It's a way long road from Marshall Texas
To the White House
For a young black woman just of
Wilcox college
recommended to Lady Bird
to be her cook and sooth LBJ's
mercurial moods and tastes for
good ole' style food along with
some cornpone bonhomie'

everywhere prejudice
no hotels to stay
no toilets to use
along the way to the Capitol back in the day
segregated all the way

stayed with the Johnson's
became part of who they were
offered up advice, some insights on
the struggle from pulpit to street
and she owned it all
never backing down or
afraid to say

the time was now for civil rights
she told him, in the halls
outspoken between dishes from toast
to roast, over coffee
she let LBJ know
silence was not her way

and when the hero died in Dallas
she did not relent or let him go his way
the prize was still unclaimed
equal rights for all, filtered like the
aroma of good dishes, she brought to them
along with pokes and laughs as she
scurried in the old West Wing

even as LBJ brings Marshall
to the hallowed court
nails the Civil Rights Act to his legacy wall
she cooked her way through it all
providing push and pie
from a soul that knew the pain of a blackened
past, that even without Martin and John, it could
not be allowed to pass
this classic moment, in her time
undone

college educated, this, Zephyr Wright
a homemaker, risk taker, opinion maker
confidante 'and force for change
even as the eggs were scrambled, the toast
buttered, and the dinners served.

Falling in Love Again

"what am I to do, can't help it"
Dietrich would intone
Softly
As if a man whispers in her ear
Walking past the Eiffel Tower
As a mist descends, as lovers
Walk towards darkness, to a sublime
Retreat
Night cloaking them, in divine embrace
Bound by a love song composed
Looking at a distant star

Romance of another time
Face to face
Not on line, no swipe left or right
Actual, not of electrons in space
When people had time to be
Together, and just wanted a safe space

I have an aging friend who always looked
Like Gable, in his prime
In our youth, we promised we would meet in Zermatt
Climb the Matterhorn together

Trek to some Xanadu, read ancient manuscripts
In the libraries
of Timbuktu

The road of a planned life
Had far too many curves
Gaping holes and ravines
Some smooth stretches, mostly
Traveled rutted paths

You know the tales of tears and woe
Marriage, children endings of volition
And, then, those of the forces unrelenting
Cancers, tumors, tremors of disease, taking
Wives, those children, and.. more

He was left alone, with partners gone
alone became loneliness
Wrote for solace, took each day as given
Gratitude became a mantra, faith kept
His hand off the revolver in his bedside
Drawer

Stumbled through or destiny revealed
A friendly face on a dating site
That caught the whimsy of an old gal
who seemed to enjoy whatever he
contemplated, which was not Kismet

Sold the place where the decades passed

Left it all at long last, with a bonfire in the
New Jersey backyard, where fumes and white smoke once
signaled
Ribs and T bone steaks
When his alarmed neighbors called the firefighters
To extinguish this flame, he shrugged, gave them beers
And wished them well, all the same

Falling in love again
Ready for the third act
Overlooking a beach, with someone else nearby
With everything behind them, prologue only
To whatever it is comes next
And, maybe we'll meet in Zermatt, yet……

Whatever Became of Red Levine

all his buddies are gone
all to tragic, but deserved ends
"Lepke" Buchalter got the chair at Sing Sing
Pittsburgh Phil, Happy Malone, Frank, "the Dasher"
Abbandando, and quiet, Buggsy Goldstein
Same chair, same place, same fate

Mostly Jews, because Lucky Luciano's enemies
Didn't know their faces, their names, or expected any
Of them of being devoted hired hands, who saw their
Work of murder, nothing more, but another job

Samuel "Red" Levine was like that
Kept a kosher house
Loved his wife and kids
Wore a yarmakule under his hat
Didn't do a job on the Sabbath
Stayed home to pray

No job was too dangerous or
Frightened Red at all
They wanted Salvatore Maranzano

eliminated, Red got the call
stabbed the old Don in the heart
and went home to dinner with the girls

He faded away, never served a day of time
shielded his life of crime
watched as they mopped Anastasia's blood
off a barbershop floor
and read the headlines of his one time friend
Bugsy Siegel catching bullets in his head
In Beverly Hills
Didn't phase him at all
Lived life quietly, observant
Eventually put away the daggers
Blackjacks and his 22
To where no one knows
Except maybe Meyer, who figured out
How to lay low, in those last years
Enjoy the ball games, bet sometimes with
a bookie, and take long dreamless naps
and never have a nightmare
Red was just doing a job, with one clear
conscience,
La Chaim.

A Still Point in a Turning World

T.S. Eliot sought it
Found its way to a page of poetry
No ascent or descent, no back and forth
Just there, where nothing moved
Frozen for a nanosecond
To savor and not be spent
A present time, fully loaded with
attention, embraced not only
observed
absorbed to soul depth
cherished, remembered,
recalled as a reason to be

and wait for another still point to come
or just go in constant search of one
more, a pause of sanity, in the calamity
that is your life

Is it that which I seek?
All these places seen
endless hikes up obscure mountains
skiing down Colorado slopes
running across the Mojave, through the

Bronx to Central park
being tossed to a mat by a sensei in a backyard
dojo in Tarzana
swimming at dawn in the sea of Galilee
surfing a break in La Jolla
finishing any race, anywhere

not the action of it, at all
the space after and between
where sitting propped against a tree
after, seems serene
or, when the book falls to carpet
and the sun warms your face, and dribble
bubbles from your open mouth, and I am
at peace, still

I know, you cannot create that moment
when the rotation suspends, it comes
when it comes, just ensues
but I've had a few, after something, fine
a strenuous exertion, challenge met, or
utter exhaustion done
yet, when I really search memory
for those moments, when my world
stood still
it was always with her head on my shoulder
with nothing else to do but be together
without a sound, or thought
and hold each other until the world
intruded again.

Sense Memory – Cold

When you take on the 'method'
And you think you can act
Visions of you as Brando or Dean
Run through you as stand up before a
Bunch of other broken down rejected
Hopefuls, about to do a scene
You can hear Stella Adler yell
"sense memory"

That's a trick you can use to unlock your
Memory and your neural pathways to
Find the exact feelings left deep inside your mind
of terror, abuse, a beating, mostly shame
and confusion that you can bring up
like emotional vomit
authentic, crass, yet, pure

I had to be cold, not of emotion or heart
Just uncomplicated cold and shiver on that stage
In an August haze, in a damp T shirt, under everyone's
gaze

Detroit came to mind
In bitter winter, wind chilled to
-10
Running before work in an Orange Philly
Flyers cap, smelling the exhausts of the
Cars, the pure stench of fumes in my nostrils
That brought some warmth

Walking down the main street in
Erie, with the "hawk" cutting through me
Off the flat lake, frozen, over dunes of
Ice, nowhere to retreat, before special fabrics,
Gore-tex and such could offer solace
Scarves and layers, for the three miles
To lecture a class in the rise of Mussolini
And have their attention, because it was
Warm in the lecture hall, and fascism had its own
appeal, and I showed some newsreels

yet, what got me shivering
yes, shivering was the recollection
of an early spring day at the third oar
of a racing shell, rowing up the Schuylkill,
before school
under grey/black skies
in the rain
feet purple, hands almost black
and my neck frozen
pulling on stroke for miles until
the turnaround

leaving the boat and running
the four miles back, soaked, purple
and black of skin

the mind knows what you went through
it is always there
hidden or locked away because you don't want
it remembered or rerun
and even deeper there are places in those
neural paths better left untouched, unrevealed
you might find something there that does not
just frighten you, but, reveals a sense of you
better lost, than brought onto some forlorn
stage

Enlarged or Reduced by Life

It is not a matter of actual
real or imposed
the forces descend regardless of
our plans declared at full voice
or
whispered

you start out determined to be
until destiny bends your will another
way
doctors become car salesmen
concert pianists butchers who play
at bar mitzvahs and in bars
mayors' and senators school teachers
playing paddleball in Boca after 35 years
keeping the peace at an inner city school

that miraculous body that could throw,
swim, wrestle and throw a Marciano right hook
reduced to replaced knees, sore arms,
surgery on colon to bladder
scraped melanoma's and morning
wood from time to time

less on demand

all of it can shrivel a man
suck the sinew dry
drain the testosterone
turn you bald, toothless, and
weak of sight

the trick is to take it all
spit at the forces, only look in the
mirror if you see the way you were
never let any of it reduce you
that spirit is still there awaiting a nudge
to emerge in full, with a declaration
that none of it, none of it has
diminished you

you are enlarged by life
survived the body blows
what happened, happened and
so
you have not turned away
or, let sarcasm and cynicism rule your
days
your authenticity is not in doubt
you have not relinquished your
purpose, just to be and survive
which is enough anyway

you have been reduced in some ways

that only matter to outsiders
your inner voice speaks
that the grandeur of life comes
when you embrace the forces
deal with them and
move on

life enlarges a man who only
sees what is next
the possibilities and will not be reduced
by life itself.

Say Goodbye to Patsy's

Midweek night in Manhattan
As the 70's come to end
Exhausted city from a decade of
Excesses
Gasoline lines
Overdoses
Overindulgences
Fears of mullahs who hold hostages
Meltdowns at nuke plants
People actually drinking the Kool Aid

So we would go to a quiet place
Shrimp scampi smell and the aroma
of pasta cooking embraced street smart guys
like us
Patsy's was just a walk from wherever we were
Been there since the war
And Joey always gave us the entire second floor
After dinners were done at 10:01

Pasquale then Joe, and his attentive
Son Sal
all Scognamillo

not mobbed up, straight
family, and everyone came
The Chairman, blessed it early on
Politicians of note and not
Al Martino, Buddy Greco, Lauren Bacall,
I sat next to Julius La Rosa as he plowed through
Lobster Oreganata, observed Bess Meyerson
fawn over her buddy Mayor Koch

pick a cliché
years take their toll
the city dies when the leadership sucks
when nobody cares anymore about
Patsy and his grandson Sal
Break their back with regulation, unjust
Specifications, and force people away
By playing king for a damn day

Patsy's is going away
To some place where people still dine
And schmooze away an evening
Far away from mid town where you can drive
and actually park, and not reach for your
holster in the dark

never would have occurred to any of us
that night
seven of us eating pasta and clams
talking about the ballerina from the Met
Monsky was screwing

the ex- ripping out Augie's heart
the payout from Bobby's bookie on the
Jets spread
All seemed forever, as the rain beat at the
windows, and the three :38's in ankle holsters
stayed put
until the rain ended, we ran out of stories and bull
and limped back to whatever we called home
never thinking as the years collided with reality
Patsy's would be gone.....

Before the Dogs Awake

If I dream I can't remember
I sleep not frightened
Battles, blood images finally gone
soaked sheets no more
yet, contorted women,unclothed
also long forgotten,lessened with a
mere drip, drip of testosterone flow
and nothing rises to meet the emerging light
as dawn becomes my reveille
except me

Dobermans across the road rest silent
at their guarded gate, protecting the guy
with one lost leg, exhausted from a night
orchestrated by their wretched cacophony

French bulls yapping through all the NFL games
as their Czech,long legged owners, go out to get
laid

Mutts down the hall scratching to get out
as their SEAL team master shouts
"shut the fuck up… shut, the fuckupforChristsake"

Quiet enough until sunrise
To contemplate emails urging
Donations, oath swearing, buying mostly
Praying for something, someone, and your own
Salvation
and, on Sunday, one encouraging contemplation
just below the one where you can get
ammo cheap

retire to the can and hope for
salvation
microwave water into tea
burn the toast black, to soothe
the tortured gut

run towards the sunrise
away from the pajama crowd
on crap patrol with Fido
and sit on a bench in the sun
until the German Shepard growls…

Can't make that Spare

It sat there churchlike on an expansive lot
of blacktop, before malls
a Sears on one side, the Tuxedo and Bridal shoppe
on the other
an emporium to the regular guy
gathering place, where contests were waged
by small packs of men in embroidered
open collar shirts, in leagues two nights a week
with 16 pound balls, two and three holed, soft leather
two toned shoes, and rosin bags tossed from man to man
between frames

thirty lanes from end to end
men in the middle, women to the right
teens and families on the left on non league
nights

life played out there between the strikes
and spares
boys on first dates, ogling girls in tight pants
men meeting their wives, that would bowl
together for the next 30 years
cranky men, overwhelmed with burdens

calmed by the collision of ball and pins
where the noise of the place, had a melody to it
that overcame the discordant pounding from
the world outside

and who could forget the night
Manny Rodriquez had one more strike
Just one to hit the perfect game
And all 30 lane went silent, we all inhaled,
Even the guys on their tenth Camel, and watched
His hook go left to right, into the pocket
And smoke and screams, and pounding ensued
Because Manny had done it, and you were there

Now 85 names, on the wall
Three guys who hit 297,298, 300
Over the last fifty years
And Big Joe Humble, was shutting it all down
Not enough business since the virus came to town

And some equity fund bought the entire lot
Raised their rent, until they could not pay
Did not give a crap about keeping them open or not
They took the pins away
Got the balls ready for resale
Pulled down the placards from the wall of fame
Left one lane open for old timers to roll a frame
Before it all goes away

I threw a 7 – 10 split

And then went after the seven to
Make the spare
Would need many more tries after
All these years
As the ball rolled between the pins
Into the emptiness
And the pin changer swept away the
7 and the ten
And no ball ever will roll down
Lane 10, again.

Just Then Awareness Comes

Routine overtakes adventure
the mundane triumphs over universal truths
petty miseries cloud your consciousness
anger flows, until it ebbs at a damn of
abject uncertainty
everything a jumble, out of and misplaced
soft thoughts for harsh pronouncements
concerning trivial disagreements outsized
by your attention to them

unsettled afternoon
driving to an exit where there is a park
where you can strip to your shorts and
run around the soccer fields, as the dark skinned
Costa Ricans clash with their hard working Honduran
counterparts
released they are into the purity of the game
the rent, and unpaid bills, and immigration screws vanished
as they play

so you run with complaints in the forebrain
arguments devised but not given
contemplating quitting, knowing you cannot

running hard for a time, using pain to forget
but not enough to erase
the concerns of this rutted life

a handsome man, who you would once say
is old, not nearly so now, perspective colored
by your own decay
is exercising with a buoyant trainer

"three up, and two slow down"
"That's it squat, keep it up"
he is slow and when he talks he
reveals the stroke stutter
and his gait, lists to the left side
his left arm frozen at his side
and I watch them, pull at rubber cords
squat, and, collapse on the trainers thigh

and the observation, pulls me away from my
self absorption
lay on my back under a cloudless sky
as the sun warms my chest, knockout sit ups
pause, and do push ups watching the man
struggle to lift water bottles over his head
no epiphany rises inside my sealed engine of a
psyche
but awareness overcomes me
and I say the 23rd Psalm

hoping in some deep recess of my being
that I will
"live in the house of the Lord forever"
Right!

Street Fights

I drift off into a memory
Uncomfortable, unnerving
Palpable
In a canvas chair, alone
Looking through the blinds
At a full moon's stare

I am fighting in the alley
or in the breezeway by Eric's
house, battling older boys bare-
chested, long armed banshees
with brass knuckles, chains, and
"Reds" swinging the Louisville slugger
With some dead players name
At my skull

Always embattled, it seems
Fighting to right some larger wrong
An attack on younger boys, defending
Some girls virginity, or the highest cause
A mother's honor
I can feel nosebleeds, busted lips, puffed up
Eyes

Washing my blood stained T – shirt, before I go home
See myself fighting from 8- 18, toughs surround me
And I never stand down
championing the unprotected in the old
neighborhood

And I touch the scars that remain
The healed bones, gnarled fingers,
And off center nose
Knowing I fought the fights
Worth fighting, about injustice,
Bullies, honor and such
And never the other skirmishes
Afraid some punk would get lucky
Punch me out, denounce and demean
My hard fought for domain
Street fights defined me then
Lessons carried with me through those years
Even, now, knowing there are still causes to champion
Punches to take and return, good men will slow
But always know when you can't back down

Drive Thru Epiphany

It is cold enough to want a warm meal
not plastered by microwaves
even though you have no cravings
never did, possessed of a unpretentious
palate, still
something prepared by someone else
reminiscent of decades gone where
the cook had a soft cheek, long neck,
and full lips of greeting after a days
work

into a line of cars by a broken driveway
where three guys are already under their blankets
eating what they dove for in the green dumpster

behind a four times regular size
Dodge Ram on monster truck wheels
Turn down the radio where Cyndi Lauper
sends out the anthem, Girls Just Wanna Have Fun"
and you imagine, Big Lou Albano, with a rubber band on his goatee
playing her distressed father

and you hope, as your bladder aches for the guy

ahead to order fast and move along
never happens
somehow the universe knows
when you are speeding and it is
slowing you down
so reflection comes or madness
ensues

50.35 it says
And it will take until dawn for it
get all made
I order a half of something
"No more halves, Sir"
Cough up a ten for a salad and a baked
Potato, with sour cream
Sit and ponder, what did I do
To repent for Lent
Everything I promised to decline lasted
a week, my awareness and consciousness
had transcended nothing

I remained as grounded, stuck, un- reconstructed
as ever
my only virtue a renewed patience
for everything
expecting nothing to go easily or my way
anymore
sending out the vibes of defeat, even here
behind the Ram and a guy with friends
and family, to handle 50 bucks in

fast food
having only myself, I moved
quickly
the gal behind me in the BMW
smiled and waved
and I sped away towards
another night with a lukewarm meal
and nobody to even say
welcome home

The Torch of Truth

Who carries it now
This torch that lights the way
To understanding, awareness of the
Righteous path, consecrate the
Grounds where intellect succeeds
And intuition weighs in supported with facts
On a scale that seeks balance
Without the heavy thumb of power,
Wealth and even
celebrity distorting, cheating it
all

into a darkness we have descended
of blame, vituperation, false claims,
angry diatribes, unproven accusations,
damning lamentations, exchanging civility
for the profane, eloquence for the vocabulary of
the gutter

Aristotle could never know
Just how low man can go to
Hold to a point of view so devoid of
truth at all or worse

to claim with utter certainty an assemblage
of lies, so obvious to a balanced few
accepted in the present milieu as undeniably
true

Hitler knew that the bigger lie could always
Overcome the truth, if the truth was hard to stomach
And didn't' elevate you
Truth, after all, requires work, to get to when you are
Struggling to survive the stranglehold of the mob
prepared to lynch you for being uncertain rather than
a zealot for their point of view

Bob Caro studied men and power, and found
"There is no objective truth, no single truth
Simple or unsimple, eternal or otherwise
No truth about nothing.. There are facts, discernable
And verifiable, and the more facts you accumulate the closer
You come to whatever truth there is… but finding the facts
Takes time.

Truth Takes Time

Who has the time to find or know it
Faces in screens, chins in chests, conversation
murdered by electronics, every view has its own
silo, where falsehoods echo off bare walls, and
no one will say hello, without a missive of hate, invectives
as the parlance, the lingua franca of the time

who carries the torch of truth?
That will incinerate the black forest of falsehoods
Burn away the poisonous plants tended by the
harbingers of hate
set fire to the hyenas who tear apart the carcasses of anyone
who dares to say there is another way
and never yield to winds of indifference
or bow to extinguish the flame

Non Fungible Tokens

Whatever smarts I had or
Can recall at all
Cannot grasp what is ahead
In far too many recesses of the
emerging brains
and when I sit on a concrete bench
contemplating what's next most of
what is happening would just never
occur to me

a moke named Beeple collects
13 years of images of stuff, not on canvas
But digitally, gives it Christies' to sell
And guarantee its unique, one of a kind
Like a Van Gogh or Picasso, but only all on line
In some cloud in digital, hyperspace
And they find a buyer named
Metakovan, yeah his code name for
69 million dollars

But it is not my Ben Franklin's but a
Cryptocurrency of the realm from ether
43,399 of them

Held in a sacred blockchain
And sold on a computer marketplace
Named for no known reason
Nifty Gateway

There is a way out there
beyond my comprehension
for men like me, who lived two early
acts without a computer, portable phone
or I pads and Tik Tok
when the technology of challenge was the
Hi-Fi in the basement, and a failing
carburetor in the Pontiac

now these digiterati are about to
open the Guggenheim
on line, where any original, verified imagery
can sell, all
non fungible tokens
and a curator will be named
Twobadour who is connected to
the billionaire, Metakovan
and Beeple becomes Basquiat

Marie Made it to 92

Jackie O shared her grief
Lost her husband to the same man
On that same day
Just 45 minutes away from
when she held JFK in her lap
Marie Tippit was home
J.D. on patrol just southwest of
downtown

He was a cops,cop
Sharp eyed enough to spot
a man who "fit the description"
of an assassin on the run
then the universe closed in on him
at 1:15 pm
he exited his patrol car and Oswald
shot him dead

Marie alone when she is told
Just another day, she thought until
everything darkened, the wealthy and
the powerful sharing the same emotions
lashed together by distorted destiny

that J.D. would go this way
and she would be a living monument to
what happened on that day

she found a way at 35
"I just couldn't figure out how
we were going to live without him"
but she did, mostly quietly, got on
with living, what else is there to do
unless you let it end you, then and there
it can be overcome, she would say,
"just get on with it, everyday

Ruby evened the score
one might suppose
lightened no burden for Marie and Jackie O
Marie outlived them all
each one in that car
Ruby, Connelly, the secret service guys
who climbed on the trunk to Jackie
all died long ago

who can measure grief
calculate the pain
understand what it actually takes to
go on, regardless of the ache and
memory of what it was like that day

Marie held on
Went forward

Asking nothing of history
knowing only she would remember J.D.
to her last day
not a mere footnote
but a true
profile in courage

Where are You?

This mind we have can confound us
imprison us in the daily grind
convince us we are miniscule
tell us to forestall it all
mire us in the long ago
reduce us to living in the past
force us to review losses, cataclysms,
errors in judgment, and not lay any
of it to rest

put a chokehold on the here and now
strangle away our ambition
asphyxiate our dreams

or, force us into tomorrow
bring worry to the fore
preoccupy our intentions for some
imagined outcome with a certain end
that requires steadfastness, resolve, and
courage
that we question we can summon before
it all ends

in the past, the mind is full of regret
resentment, anger, cowardly acts,
inaction, and despair
over what might have been
the damage done to everyone else
and the deep gash in your soul

and that future consciousness
turns you anxious
aware of disabilities, inherent flaws,
and if you have the stamina, heroic nature
to get there, to what is awaiting you, that
your mind promises
after all

there are always forces that can shift you from a
path, but nothing matters if you can't see that the
master of your consciousness is you
in the presence of the moment
it is yours to direct and be
the "silent knowing within"
it requires no lobotomy, no genetic cure,
only recognition that you are the guiding
spirit of your own direction
you cannot let it drift towards ancient memories
unlit corridors to a sarcophagus of buried flaws

or live the fear of future demands that bring worry
you can't achieve it all

Presence is all it requires and to not
Give a damn

Say Goodbye to Western Civilization

That's what my bro network, buddy, Danny
muttered after he watched two women, on a huge
bed, sing and pretend to sex play before millions on
television, in prime time, at some awards show
Robust, large bosom and bottom phenoms
From nowhere to the top of the charts
Black, proud, and loud artists with stage names
Cardi B and Megan Thee Stallion

To old cranky men, and most of the sane world
It looked like two lesbians making love, or two of
a threesome waiting for the lone and lucky man
not soft core, but, prurient, hard core porn
you know it when you see it, said Justice Potter
Stewart

But was it more than titillation, but a sign of the
demise of Western Civilization?

You read Gibbon when you're too young to
Know things rise and fall, gladiators, wealth in the hands of a few
Freedom given to but a few, mores shattered, rules gone awry
only the haves, have everything and the rest only comply or

die
Toynbee is an acquired taste, rarely taught anymore
Studied 26 civilizations all had the same essential downfall
They committed suicide, he claimed, which got him into the
Historians hall of fame,
They bled to death from self-inflicted wounds, first they decayed,
developed historical Alzheimer's, and were so weak when opponents
clamored for power, the elites morphed into cowards

And Buddha came to us, to late
For any of my ilk to get that nothing is permanent
Good or evil, it all ends
And you with it, at a juncture you cannot design
or devein

worse signs than gyrating singers
in G strings on a bed
when what passes for inspiration is
degradation, when perversity is blessed by
diversity
and everything once cherished is corroded
can you hear the walls crumbling as the Temple is destroyed?

Ode to Spring

It is not tripping over purple hills
blowing across fields of grain
with rosebuds in her hair
warm breezes deterred by artic lows
bringing chills to old men eating canned
soup, and burnt toast in empty flats
everywhere

small dogs yapping throughout the day
big bottomed women walking Dobermans
muscled men picking up crap of dogs they would
be ashamed to show to their father
symbolic of what it takes to appease the gal who
cooks and cleans, and satisfies what passes for carnal
stimulation

delivery trucks always backing up with the annoying
sound of a safety beep, as if the whole world was in a
bad French movie, with that sound running through the
street of a cop car chasing a heroin dealer
sirens moan, EMT ambulances off to set a leg, adjust a

neck brace, take a dead teenager on his ride to the
the morgue, after a street race gone wrong, for him and
five of his bros'

lunatics rule
massage parlor women gunned down
people attacked for being who they are
cherry blossoms bring murder and assault
for having skin of a certain hue
disgruntled man decides to bury his wife alive
a Governor tells an aide, he would mount her
if she was a dog
the homeless guy around the corner sleeps with his
face in his vomit until noon

a season of renewal
shielded behind frowns
grunts, and one sentence dialogues
replacing conversation and connection
untouched millions, unhugged masses
touching elbows, fearful of what comes in
the next breath

So, I flee for solace
Seeking out the devoted avocet, and its
tiny flock, piercing sand with its beak for
grubs
watching sandpipers scurry
as ducks shimmy to deep waters
and the gulls come energetic and full

throated
three fisherman cheer off shore as one
gets dinner on a once untouched hook
and a bent over woman, pulled along by
a spotted black on white great Dane says
"good morning to ya"

Maybe it won't be that bad an equinox
After all…..

You Don't Need a Fire to Burn a Book

Guttenberg could not know
or imagine that all that is printed
could be immolated on a caustic
whim by the wave of a hand, a mere
grunt from men in power
to set aflame some tome to
eradicate the words, turning thoughts
to ash

hoping that no idea can be sustained
once the mob knows the words are
to be defamed, the authors gutted of ideas
stripped and raped tossed into a bonfire
forever shamed enough to never write
again

blasphemy, apostates, philosophy of any other
point of view, and, of course, everything written by
any Jew, submitted to a Fahrenheit high enough to
incinerate, as Pope's and their inquisitors laughed
as carts of Talmud's passed,
novels, science, comic tales, over centuries created
then destroyed, never ending flame, the smell of

print and paper rising into the nostrils of hate
until the fumes were of flesh and sinew
bodies, with souls exchanged for mere pages

no torches now
electrons, and algorithms
aseptic arbiters of what you read
access and distribute
ruled by cyber- tyrants, who have gotten rich
selling everything, but not ideas they do not hold

dare you write a book that claims
transgenderism has its flaws
that all lives deserve consideration
or socialism is a crock
not merely be knocked
or mocked
but erased, in an environmentally pure way
no carbon footprint, no ash, nothing at all
whatever you wrote is just dead

no vote taken, no survey needed
the elites decide
you did not abide
too many thou must nots now
no one will ever see what you created
if
you are Dr. Suess and drew a cartoon wrong
mention a protected minority group in a

negative way
claim a cop killer named Assata is harbored
in Cuba, and should not in Black Live Matters
hall of fame
equity lens' are flawed and distorted
cops need to stay
from each according to ability to each
according to their need is
socialism
race is a social construct not based on
science and DNA
systemic racism is a slogan for division
and skin color cannot be permitted to determine
right from wrong

You could see the torch a coming
Watch the flames arise
Pray for salvation and in time
prevail, an idea on fire cannot be
extinguished, in the minds of good
people
but
if the word never rises
is never seen or heard
then what of our thoughts opposed
to the tyranny of this insidious thought
control

who will take on the
pernicious censors who

sit in cubicles, and axe no faggots to
burn the books, have turned their torches
into electronic gates through which
no viewpoints pass but their own

Get Over It

Is everything, just about us?
No matter how vast the topic
National debt, travel to Mars, faceless
protein burgers, that new breast cancer
test, electric cars, no drip mascara, a new
downtown bar, reparations for slavery, micro-
aggressions
sent through the prism of self
our own perception screen
mostly I and me

listening barely for insight
rarely with empathy
searching for equity
that one story trumps another and
is lasting in time

self absorption, attachment to what
is, overdoing, overplaying any of it
rising in importance, out of proportion
slights become affronts
maladies, cast as chronic ills
misgivings inflated to utter dismay

shame prevails, after anger flows down
the psychic drain
on everything we see as lost
and we live,too often, walking
around in despair, beaten, overcome
with dismay at what becomes each
day

yet
ranunculus explode
across fields of purple, red and yellow
desert landscapes are flush with orange
pelicans soar and dive as they have for a million
years or so
a heron stands gazing at a horizon on one leg
a lizard eats a bug
an old man soaks in the sun and puffs a new
cigar

a beautiful, woman passes with dark hair
a baseball cap, and the lean body of a volleyball
player, long legs, in shorts
except as she approaches
one is gone, thigh locked into a prosthesis
and she smiles as she passes me

and I am self conscious
cannot look away
enthralled by her poise and steady gait
and taken away from my utterly inane

focus on biography to
awareness of another's journey
and fight to accept what is and
just go on
and smile at a stranger

Defenestration

Always been windows
ledges
moats and hard ground below
where the strong throw the weak
away, mostly dead before
strangled and stabbed
but then
others tossed alive, so they can
contemplate the dive to sudden death
deserved or not
defenestrated as might makes right
or
so un wrapped to toss themselves away
rather than suffer torture, starvation, loneliness
and utter decay

Jezobel had a eunuch who could not stand her
anymore
in Prague whoever they threw away started a
war that day that lasted 30 years, until there was
no one left to toss and they all cut their losses
and signed the Treaty of Westphalia in 1648
James ll of Scotland fame threw the Earl of Douglas

onto the hard ground below
and the St. Bartholomew Massacre rose to unique acclaim
as the naming rights go, Huguenots thrown, Catholics as well
no one caring exactly who was going straight to hell
Robespierre's brother threw himself to the ground to avoid
the guillotine, and failed … in pain and crippled
the blade was welcomed

the Red Guard roamed the streets for Mao
gathering the unfaithful, purging anyone smart enough
to know the little Red Book was a scam
dangled Deng Pufang, until he cried and dropped him
on his skull, son of Deng Xiaoping could not save the boy
intent they were on defenestration of everything anti- Mao
so now here we are again
the holders of the grail threatening all
who do not know their way, throwing alternative ideas
away
statues fall, books banned, buildings renamed,
people shamed for past transgressions, lies created to
destroy and maim, other bothersome voices
first the ideas pile up, then the bodies, eventually,
everyone closes their windows to silence the screams of intolerance

All My References Are Dead

or unable to remember
synapses and neurons shot
with amyloid plaque, lewy bodies
Parkinson shivers and distorted imaginations
on meds and ventilators, Gene breathes inside
an oxygenated chamber

those with genetic gifts
some who managed to contain despair
or drank enough Johnny Walker to ward off
despair, inflammation, frightened away invaders, and
married younger woman, who were good for more
than their prostrates

others still above ground have
disowned the past, recovered sanity
and gave up being a master of the universe
and why not from the view of Park Avenue
provided by a current wife, a widow
with a few million bucks, and family to despise
on holidays no less
or

cruising Palm Beach in a pink golf cart
picking up the misses after she plays
Mah Jong

This HR person wants to know, nicely,
"you have the experience, for certain,
But, we'd like to check your references"
And I sigh, knowing I have it all, save for that
precious essence, good as 18k gold,
youth
long gone

So I can only say:
"Most are gone, a few remain, I'll
get you a list, right away, if you're serious
about going forward, OK?"

only to never hear from her again.

Why Did He Kill Them

Everyone asks and wants to know
how could he just shoot them all
without compassion or pause
pull a trigger and slaughter them all

always been that way
believing there must be a cause
a motivation behind it all
not just madness, lunacy,
derangement always there and expressed
before
killing cats, torturing dogs, pulling wings off
butterflies and birds,
doing horrible things to little girls on backyard
swings, scribbling endlessly, sitting for hours alone,
afraid to answer a phone
not able to sit through dinner, throw a baseball to Dad,
laugh or cry

why do we wonder if there is a larger purpose
some imagined major blow that only murder will
unfold
that comes from some polemic, philosophy

or belief, sullied, crapped upon, or defamed by the
target of their grief
a motivation that can be explained, that channels
impulse control lost, into a need for a measured acclaim
that can only be achieved by sending bullets into organs
and brains, obliterating all of them by the same hand
that rises in victory over a floor of blood

why does the why matter
if it is ever really true
choice a delusion, a disorder mix them in
a psychic brew, sprinkle in ideology, a tortured
belief in who is to blame
obvious targets, never really changed
blacks, politicians of every type, inequities,
poverty, obsessions of all types, sexual muses
imagined, never real, autocrats, plutocrats,
wayward democrats, and even a Republican who
freed the slaves, or fought off Gorbachev

lost, distant, angry, disconnected
unreachable, devoid of consciousness,
awareness and reflection
so in pain, only released as the
bullets fly, bringing release, solace
without remorse
just another "bad day" they usually
retort

a man in body armor walks into King Sooper's grocery

with five guns and a rifle
kills a cop and nine others
and Boulder mourns

another,known to be lost and under care
enters a massage parlor he went to hoping for happy endings
that they did not offer
killed 8 from place to place

was one a hate crime, the other not?
Isn't it all hate, anger, despair, utter and
so painful, no one can bear it
pounding inside, until everything aches
until they are overcome with one thought
that the deed will be done, and they will
be free, and it all will become calm
but never does cease for anyone, but the dead

Welcome to Potemkin Village

He was one lover, of a woman
who had men on demand
sent armies to sustain an empire
and was not easily wooed or impressed
Potemkin knew if he could find a way to
lift her spirits, ingratiate her sense of power
and divine right
he might extend his time in Catherine the Great's
bed for some more nights

Russia beat down the Turks in Crimea
tenuously coveted the land
so Gregor constructed towns of only facades
that she would see along the way to
visit those Crimean towns
from her carriage, through the cordons of
men, she could not know, that it was all just a shell
game, put on by Potemkin to convince her she
had conquered well

no noble purpose now
no throbbing heart and pulsating organs
nothing to protect or hide, but the truth behind

the fake walls
of distortions, half measures, cowardice, and
unseemly political maneuvering
so vile, despicable
that it must be cloaked, so the Potemkin's
of this time can raise and move the city as they please
to keep us all from turning them out for the liars
they have become

children from other places living in veritable cages
tent cities of families stranded abandoned by noxious
policies
tons of cocaine, fentanyl, and marijuana sitting on docks
as they deny the war on drugs is lost
inner cities abandoned, neglected for a generation
and downtowns cesspools, outdoor toilets for
the homeless, addicted, distracted, and insane

Potemkin knew what he was about
his purpose simple and clear
his subterfuge was quaint
not like it is now
who will take the wrecking ball to it all?

Hey, There is a Soul in There

Coarse poets treat them horribly in
verse, stanza, and memory
calling them by their orifices
their entry points of holes designed for other
things, except for one that is destination, center of
sensation, and deliverer of progeny wanted and not

to which they bloviate about, endlessly
of what they gave up for
surrendered to
whipped by it, lured by it, the
p word, operated by a c word
who manages to put up with them
for a few bucks, a safe place to be, and
companionship, if even from a hairy, thick
waist beast

courtesans, ladies of the night, call girls
priced high and low
income makers, earners for the mob
cartels, pimps and brothels
in windows from Amsterdam to Frankfurt
above bars in fanned rooms from St Nicholas to San Juan

walking streets by the Port Authority, sipping martini's
at the Sky Bar, where they glitter like Vegas below

they all have stories
mostly of woe, rarely what they want to be
or thought they would become
tricks add up, the life they wanted,distorted by
the exchange of fates, and cash for friction, the
feel of a soft body under a calloused hand, and a
brief pause in the give and take of the world, you
want to forget, but can avoid, as the in and out
ensues, and subsides

all the madmen who call them names
know without them, life can be lonely as hell
these whores, you say, who you curse from day to day
all have souls, you know, and they come equipped with it
and it cries out to them, when you are not there
and you could pray for it to be repaired from the
gash you give it, as you try to heal your own.....

The Hand of Pluto

on Proserpina's thigh
holding her tightly as she struggles
to release herself from a fate offered by
the Gods
to be taken to the underworld
to be raped and held by Pluto

the three headed dogs bark
at her feet
overwhelmed by the pure strength of her
captor, who will not relent
the destiny secured of a woman sent to hell
only to escape and be raped again

a tale desired by wealthy men
patrons of arts and lore
who compelled young men of extraordinary
skills to mount marble with hammer and
chisel
and
reveal these forms with impeccable
precision
in times, dark

for everyone but the rich
the powerful, the churched,
and the anointed
superstition, disease and plague,
books burned, new ideas turned away
no Jews in Spain or England
but those will sublime, otherworldly skills
did more than survive

at 23, Gian Lorenzo Bernini
took to that stone, and found Pluto there
capturing Proserpina
sensual, ominous, subtle in the curve of a finger
the position of her breast, her anguish
so startling, you can almost hear her scream

ability collides with will
art as transcendence
even in the worst of times
beauty reveals itself

On The Razor Wire

The hummingbird hovers over the razor wire
Concertina on the chain link fences
Keeping out or us in at dawn
Not a sound, between semi's rolling by to
Eastern places, F-18's still grounded
Awaiting young pilots scrambling eggs
Before they scramble

Only the humming birds' wings airborne
A morning mantra, brings pause
Before the battle of a day begins
Skirmishes with the unhappy, underpaid
Chin down collection of malcontents
Sullen, shark eyed, resigned to lives
Where no wings flutter carrying them towards
Dreams, wishes or any purpose

All of us on that razor wire
Afraid to land, for but a moment
Knowing that a slip of mouth, a vacant stare,
Into the wrong eyes, a laugh caught after an
Improper punchline
Can lacerate us

Even impale us on the
Sharp edge of how we exist
Subsist, pretend to not care
Eat our lunches, talk less, say nothing more
Than what a nice day we are all having
Knowing it is a damn lie

The hummingbird floats
And just is…
A purity of nothing more than
The here and now
No subtext, next or then
Only now

The semi obliterates the sound of her wings
The across the lot yells
Where the fuck is that fork lift"
You want to crawl back into the car
And head anywhere
And you could cry, if you could, but the razor wire sends you
To the time clock and the workday

Easter Sunrise

The sun always rises
clouded some years and not
ultimate metaphor for any resurrection
for each of us
Nunc Coepi
Now I Begin
Psalm 77:10 mostly unknown
It implores us
If I should Fall even a thousand times
I will say, immediately,
Nunc Coepi (Nunk Che pee)

As believers say on mountain tops
He has Risen
Most saying it in their cars, at home
Somewhere, frightened away by the rules
Of our later day Roman emperors
Imperious, protectors of themselves
Afraid of the contagion of free will
Forcing us away from churches, and that
Sunrise, to let their codes of pandemic
protection play out, aborting free souls from
worshiping in peace, offering prayers of redemption

to Christ

still Nunc Coepi
unchained, screw them, and their
unscientific crap, its about control and
nothing more than that

a boy walks in a marine layer fog and
yells, as though he was in a crowd
"I like it here, but, if it doesn't go my way soon
I'm gone"

A tall women in short shorts
Has her legs entwined by her three dogs
and talks to them as though they understand
how to unwind her

an old woman in a electric chair
speeds down the boardwalk to keep up
with her lab, who is chasing after a grey great
Dane, and the guy who feeds her morsels of
Hamburger
Two girls strip to thongs at the pool
Amp up George Strait and laugh at
everything

an ex NFL back, now a pastor
crawls out of a casket on the pulpit
and delivers his sermon on redemption
while a rock band plays behind him

four children dressed in the days pastels
toddle behind their mother, perfectly appointed
in an old fashion way, enter a church where
the mass has much to say
about hope, and resurrection, and faith

I hear the footsteps behind me
And the sun is breaking through
I pull aside as two gals, in pink and green
shorts, power by me, and their pigtails sway
and all deep thoughts dissolve into this
Nunc Coepi

Filling the Holes

A man sees a hole
And he fills it if he can
even if he did not dig it
from the earliest beach days
at a neighborhood park
or a backyard, if you were lucky enough to have
one, fill in the dog's hole
bury something secret and dear
pretend only you know where it might be
after all the years pass

constantly filling holes
getting paid to do it, on road crews
to pay for the fall semesters
shirtless over black top, patching potholes
on a gig arranged by uncle harry with the
alderman
put some cash in your pocket and generated an
awesome tan, that added to your appeal at the shore
those wayward summer days

easy enough to patch them with grit and
muscle

until you fill the primal entrances
of those girls, women, wives, and lovers
repeatedly, and hopefully forever, until your
wood is consumed in the fire of a passion hole
or just burned out
not so, the less pleasant ones that come with time
as people you wanted around die away
in drunken stupors, heroin od's, just bad luck,
bad genes, and all at risk behaviors, or just
loss, of girlfriends who dropped you, friends
who betrayed, and everyone who sought to diminish
you, kill your spirit, before it could rise inside,
ridicule, deride, denigrate, and not abide by what you were
or might become

and it all left a hole or two inside

some filled it with booze, bad habits, wanton desires
and mostly avoidance of what it was doing to your insides
as grief delayed, and tears withheld, knotted your emotions
until you screamed into the night

nothing you could do would sew it up
and these holes expanded every year
no diversion provided stiches, not a large spliff,
LSD, dames from Teaneck to Kankakee, chocolate bars,
or marathon runs
no matter, the holes remained
of those you have to admit to loved
and are gone, by death or choice all the same

the holes remain
until you face it down, hear the wind of shame
and heartache blow frigid through you
until you shiver, fever, and almost die
facing it now, finally
there is nothing more you can do
but go on…..

What the Trail Knows

Here I am on my ass
again
on a mountain trail, just a second before
scanning the scenery, gazing at Mexico,
fantasizing, a beach in Rosarito, and a long legged
woman, who speaks Spanish and only that

mind afloat on a trail that required my full attention
knowing better, jolted to awareness that each stride
required attention, scrutiny
once put aside
ended in this

a bruised, bleeding and purple knee
road rash on my right hip
sand and stones coating an elbow bleeding
bright red, a shoulder of gravel and dust
attempting and failing to roll with the fall
from a mere single rick, uncovered and
unseen, with a gash above the right eye
worthy of a right hook from Marciano

I pinch it hard to stop the flow of it to my

lips, as I spit in disgust
At knowing better and acting wrong

The trail knows
speaks to you in unsubtle ways
moderate your strides
pace yourself wisely over ruts and stones
accelerate at your own peril
When what seems smooth ahead
is mostly not, a fiction you create that
does not respond to the path as it
Is
but as you wish it to be

everything about moving forward
going fast or slow
depends as much on the trail and path as your volition
which has its limits
There is a reality there beneath you
always is, in fact
avoided by the headstrong
allowing reverie to overtake attention
Defy the rocks, the debris
tempt the forces as you neglect to
see what is ahead
Then suffer when you fall
on your head, and land on your ass
with no one to blame and curse
but you, and your unvarnished
hubris..

One Swallow to Forget Everything

Plato imagined it
There must be a Hell
or
Someplace where all the assholes dwell
some to stay eternally and suffer
eternal pain
and others, he hoped would be cleansed
reincarnated and continue to carry the
human flame

but you could not go
unless you threw off the burden of
memory, all of it, expunged
by a simple act of swallowing the water from
the spring of the river of Lethe
and every single thought worthy, or
frightening gone
not exonerated from the guilt but
it is just not there
and without memory, he thought
once again you are free

where is that spring

after all these years to
release the choices, evil voices,
indulgences, indecisions, bad ones,
broken bones, hearts, and lost souls
including yours

lying to parents over girls and fights
falling in love, pretending they loved you
being distant, diffident, father
driven by ambition, achieving little
losing more
kitchen table tongue lashings, tears
on display, empathy in short supply
burying children, and friends way before
their time

calculating loss over addition
fear triumphing offering limited
horizons, that reach always within a grasp
until you went further and failed
again and again
missed payments, mortgage due, credit
rating a joke
lost the house, blew the savings
worked every day, until muscle turned
to bone, lips thinned, and you couldn't
whistle or spit

there must be a sign somewhere
along life's road, even to there

that will point to a turn
that says
"Lethe Spring, next exit"
And I will put my lips to the flow
Take a swallow or two
and be on my way to
another place, where what I thought I might
become, might just happen….

The Only Answer is…………

I've met the men in search of answers
off to some distant Shangra La'
guys named Sheldon and Malcolm
converted to Ram Dass and Amenhotep Ra
fellows who after lectures dropped peyote,
rolled a long reefer, or tripped on LSD
after the Big Q
what is the meaning of it all…to me

same dudes argued with their wives
endlessly
ran home to have dinner with their mothers
feared their father's wrath, even when they
were 47
confronted office mates, fought the corporate
battles, mouthing off in pursuit of money, mistresses,
and convincing themselves it all was and for the
realization of their dreams

never stopped to ponder
what outcome might evolve from the
rants, erratic moves, shouts and screams
not confronting for a moment

"what do you want out of this"
Outcomes, that you can foretell
Without wizardry

Will this argument lead to understanding
This anger to accommodation
A night in bed with Julia fill the void of
a failed marriage
going to work on Sunday, advance anything but
your distance from your kids
never praying, fill the hole in your soul

simple enough to consider
what you want to happen
the outcome you desire
reverse engineer decisions, think action
through, prepare for what might happen
consequences known and not
weigh the costs and benefits
as if you were off to war

a battle it is you see
of how effective you can be
but who takes the time
breathes before you mouth off
pauses before you punch
sits in the car for ten beats and not
just gun it and speed away?

Outcomes you can control

Lest the forces come into play
But without any consideration you
Have no hope or plan
And everything can drift away
on an ocean of uncertainty

so don't take a steamer to Bombay
fly to Bhutan
eat nuts and grass
pop pills and push stuff up your ass
take a damn moment and say what
do I want out of this, and how do I get there
on what matters to you each day

or failing all of that, if you just want to
play a roulette life
say "I don't give a shit", and suck up what comes next…

Out of Nothing

There was a void until there wasn't
zeptoseconds pass, multitudes of muons
collide
seemingly nothing metastasizes, accelerates
and populates the nothingness, expanding
to perceived infinity
creation at its purest, done by the unknown
creator, the ultimate artist on a universal
canvas of matter dark and not, forces seen and
measured, mysterious and elusive
out of nothing

strong, weak, gravity,
electromagnetism and another
force, unforeseen, of a particle's
ebb and flow
that only smart guys in white coats
in Europe somewhere can know
as their cigarettes recede down their
yellow knuckles, as electrons scatter at
the speed of light, in chambers they
made to watch over, instead of I Love Lucy
reruns, on cold Nordic nights

all other blank places seem mundane
Hemingway's white bull, Michelangelo's untouched
mined marble slab, Picasso's canvas, your sperm in her egg
unless you see his creation as physics, not design
cosmic luck without volition
random colliding chaos, without a sentient plan

from nothing something
is creation, you do it
so does Manny who makes cabinets
Turko making violins
Grace and her outdoor painted landscapes of the Cape
Sylvia who sells her jewelry shaped like stars
Jacko and his murals of dead men
Even Ramon and Esther, making fish tacos, in their truck
by the fire station

even so many writers cum poets
imagined men with something to say
or compulsion more likely to pretend
ideas, fulminations of value to someone
as much as some distant rocky planet a hundred
billion light years away
or of no value at all
except to be, revealed from nothing
filling in a white space, with no
expectation of anything more
than a way to pass the time,
pretending any of it matters
at all

Just One Day is All

What if for just one day
judgment
would be suspended
old Testament style, leave it all to
some higher power, pick your favorite
deity or cosmology and then
shut up

Vladimir leaves old Joe alone
the Serbs forget there are Croatians
that junta in Burma, leaves the Rohingya alone
Beijing let's the Uyghurs in Xinjiang walk in the
market in Urumqi
the Sunni's give the Shia a day of praise

let go of
she's too fat
her boyfriend is a dick
that fast food window is too slow
all he wants is, you know
I'm so tired of my bosses bullshit
she needs to get a life
he thinks it's so funny, but it's not

what a cheap SOB, driving around in his BMW
she never listens, I just don't matter
can't she pronounce Nevada, right just once
he married such a bitch
is that all she ever wants?

Just for one day
Suspend it all, see what happens to you
And me, and this world of doom, vituperative
words of annihilation, pending inflation,
unemployment, misinformation, useless contemplation
spirit crushing, turning dreams into one long sleepless night
wondering why, you are always being judged by someone

the grand inquisitor is within
pulling us apart, chronicling the gaps
between what we want to be and actually are
enough pain there, bathed in fear and shame

just a day away from the forces
just one day when no one can say
"you're not good enough" Because you are, we all are …..

If Life Could Only Be Like Basketball

On a summer afternoon in South Philly
on a black asphalt court
with five other guys, half court
and six others after the far basket

heat rises from the court, catches the
humidity, you want to be skins to their
shirts, before fancy water bottles with caps,
just you, your sweat, and that one working fountain
where you waited in line until the big guys had their
fill

you'd sit on your butt and hope to be picked for a game
a small driving guard, was your only name, and you
gave it your best stern stare, pretending to not care
but you wanted to get picked, so you played hard
and practiced every day, bouncing that ball until
it became your background sound, from house to school
to playground

then we'd play
like we all were in the NBA
pretending, in reverie to be Wilt from West Philly

Russell or the Big O
Channeling Bradley, West, or even Cousy with
Jumps and hooks
dribbling with intensity, passing hard and fast
hoping the game would just last, over and again
until dark proclaimed the end of the game
unless the lights were fixed
and you could get the last trolley home

young men play
as if it's the NBA
committed it would seem to live out
those boyhood dreams
captured by the moment
without disruption or a single care
other than to score, sweat and triumph
on that black asphalt court
for nothing more than bragging rights
or not
without wonder or worry if
such commitment to anything else would bring
them the bliss, of a jump shot
from the top of the key, that is all net…

What The Crow Knows

There is a rolled up bag on the ledge
by the funeral home
in the back where the hearse drivers
sit in old canvas chairs, as the services
commence

and up there on the fence
crows sit, usually quietly almost
reverently, vocalizing now and again
at morning or when Augie comes out
and throws the crumbs from his bag of
Fritos by his chair

It's slow this day
one long run from the beach to
Forest Lawn, a big procession
All the cars gone
Manny's left his McDonald's bag rolled up
With something left inside from what passes
As his breakfast meal

Six crows stay on the wire
one sweeps in without a sound

picks at it tentatively
accelerates his play
until the bag is frayed and he claws
it open, in a studied way

then by instinct, guile or damn good
luck
finds uneaten edges of an egg McMuffin
then strands of potato
more egg, and a half eaten bun
and pecks at it, with a staccato beat
until it all is done

cranes his heads
points his beak towards the sun
nods to his wire hugging buddies
and offers a single crow, as he
flies to Augie's chair, craps white
and flies away

Manny rolls the casket to the pall bearers
making a buck, not wondering if it means
much, or judging if it's a good day or not
doesn't take much, really to satisfy a man
passing his day bringing the dead to hallowed
ground
or a crow, focused on its task to
uncover its
morning meal.

Is This Really Love?

It winds up on every man's list
written or not
to love and be loved
uncertain how to achieve it
can it be demanded
commanded from an outside force
imposed by others to be obeyed
or does it just ensue?

Hormones race from balls to brain
Bathing men in that ejaculated afterglow
Easily mistaking it for something more
than friction

imagining the coupling a chapter in a well worn
fiction, read by flashlight under covers with
glossy renditions of mons and breast, passionate
kisses, everywhere
leading to a coupling that would last

reality does not savor the carnal as the
mundane, back and forth of ordinary life
replacing the ins and outs of bedroom fame

the clouds of infatuation bringing a thunderstorm
of domestic rain, drenching dreams and flooding
the road you thought you'd follow, washed away

you considered it love
giving everything for her and them
working until ten, putting up with the
chasm between what you wanted and what you got
at work, with your parents, kids, and, of course,
her
who you thought actually loved you too
until you took a hard look at it, one exhausted
night, after everyone stopped coughing, complaining,
and watching some screen, and it was actually silent at
3:20 am

Somewhere between those passionate nights
having the children, paying the bills, and dinner without
an argument about, mostly money, and not enough of
anything you wanted, it appears
to most men

there is what they hoped for and wanted
and what they have
and an accommodation is made, and
then another, and another
until,whatever happiness you might have expected
vanishes
just leaves your mind and is no longer on
you silent list of what you want to stay above

ground
and you still love, but it's a long one way street
with no exit signs
and you drive along, with the radio turned up loud
so you can't hear the sound of anything, especially
your thoughts
and pretend everything is fine
when your soul knows its not
and no man spends the time
in tears…

Wind of Change

Churchill declared it an Iron Curtain
Foster Dulles dubbed it the Cold War
JFK opined "Ich bin ein Berliner"
Reagan demanded to Gorbachev
"tear down this wall"

And, as time passes, some things are
turned right, not often, but after years
of strife, the moral tale ends in freedom
or more of it, than before
and poets write of it
as do the real poets of our time
rock stars and musicians

Klaus Meine
Sits on a bench along the Moskva river
after his Scorpions play to
300,000 Russians at Lenin Stadium
And a ballad enters his psyche
"Die Idee dazu ist mir in der USSR gekommen,
als ich in einer Sommernacht im Gorky
Park Center, saB und auf die Moskwa
Geblickt habe."

The idea came to him while sitting in Gorky Park
one summer night, looking at the Moskva River

so he wrote, without pretense or deeper
consideration
"I follow the Moskva
Down to Gorky Park
Listening to the wind of change"

Lyrics from a force of inner knowing
approaching genius, defining the end of
one era and the beginning of another
Pure thoughts, unexpurgated
Haunting, melodic, poetic

Until, the new age spits up a
A writer after notoriety, regardless of the truth
Now equipped with his very own mouth orange to
spew whatever, it is that will grow his fame
and claims the CIA wrote the song, and put it into
Meine's hands and out his mouth

Rumor only, purely balderdash
No matter, when there is no retaliation
Lies are cast as true, or dubbed "maybe's" for
Prurient delights, filth masquerading as insight,
anything to grow a following, everything a joke
on someone

no place for deeper themes, action without venal
purpose, transcendent thoughts, words painting
vivid pictures in your mind, capturing a moment
in a phrase, a guitar solo bringing a stadium to tears,
a faint whistle, declaring the end to a dark, cold age
and the emergence from despair

the end of liberty
will always be when
the noise of rumor and lie
drowns out the
melody of truth

let your balalaika sing
what my guitar wants to say/

Finally

106 years
Finally now
Ole Joe admitted
The Turks back in the day
when the Ottoman empire reigned
systemically murdered every Armenian
they could find, before their Muslim
caliphate slid into a well deserved
decline

their was no name for it
named it genocide
finally
where they rounded up the men
tortured them, killed them all anyway
whether they confessed to lies of
conspiracy or not

then they herded the old and lame
infirm and women and children to
desert camps, where they figured out
ways to kill them all
but not before

they died of thirst, starved,
burned alive in groups,
raped repeatedly
piled severed heads and posed
for pictures for the guy back home
and when they ran out of ways
to murder a million and a half
took the children out in boats
and threw them into the water
and drank and laughed as they drowned

all to Turkify the peninsula
rid it of Armenians
open the way for the rise of a Muslim
bourgeois
finally to say
it was, what it was
genocide, and no apologies
to a nation of Erdogan's who still
say,
"they died, but not in a systematic way"

A lance corporal heard of it all
With his pit bull, Little Fox
his only companion, Fuchi
as he fought for Germany in that First World War
still years away from consolidating his hatred
for all Jews
until
finally he knew

the world would stand by
as he exterminated whomever he wanted to

Ole Joe knew it was genocide
So did LBJ, JFK, Reagan, both Bush's
The big O, and even,self defined tough guy,
the Donald
It took 106 years for Joe to say
the Ottoman Turks killed
A million and a half Armenians
systemically murdered them to
Ethnically cleanse the region for no
other reason, than they were who they were
and pray for them, for all of them long gone
Finally…..

The Perfect Day Illusion

It's eluded me for most of my days
as the curves and bumps occupied my
energy, eyes on the prize of the dutifully
required stops, never missing an exit for
career, love, marriage, children, falling into
potholes, running of the cliffs of sanity into
a rocky abyss
only to find my way back again, to the same
places, over and over
often without reflection, refusing recollection
never knowing that a day could be just so

perfect in form
function only to fulfill that illusion of
well being, and pure exhalation of every
bottled up stress and tribulation
cleansing breath, awaiting the inhalation of
contentment

elusive day of everything or
just enough to say
gladdened to have awakened at dawn
with the hope that a day can be crafted

untouched by the forces and lived robustly
without a tentative stroke
stoked to do whatever it is that declares
you are here, above ground for another go
at it

a woman with a limp and a green scarf
on roller blades says hello
you smile and mumble a greeting
you come up slowly on two gals
with Olympian legs, tan smooth, hairless

the pink moon lingers behind morning clouds
the sun rises on the turn around, four out and
four back,
the woman have returned from their rowing across the bay
and turn their hoses away, as you amble by, and chatter
loudly about boyfriends and food

I read three papers
old school
turn off the phone, vow to be silent until
Sunday
Drive to the car wash, knowing rain is expected
Tuesday, but not believing it
Drive slowly past the surfing breaks, bikini women
And stop to listen to dogs bark, as they run free
Into the ocean

Watch some golf tournament from Louisiana

Catch Brad Kesolowski win at Talladega after his
Partner Joey Logano, flips over in flames in overtime
Read a book on 2034, and the imagined horrors of
World War lll with China, barely adverted

Eat some crap from 7/11
Enjoy some 99 cent cookies
Finish the book in bed
Laugh, without reflection, at Cosmo, Elaine, Jerry
And George

Not a bad day
But perfect, probably not
Indolent, undirected, misbegotten
perhaps,
But perfect, hardly
Still enough to sustain, the illusion that a better one is coming.

When Will Love Return

If it ever was there at all
Anywhere
Requiring nothing of or from you
At birth
Out of love or was it fealty, circumstance
Tradition, religion, societal expectation
Some devotion, commitment to see things
Through
Mothered and fathered hearing
The divine utterance
"I love you"
on occasion at proper times and intervals

when you needed support
were withered by competition
missed most goals and were often
in transition
a motherly stare, and an outreached hand
accompanied by an overcooked brisket
"you, ok, honey, love you"

Testosterone rising from scrotum to brain
thoughts generated by the limbic system and

not your forebrain, and gushed out of you claims
of love and devotion, that lasted until you got
laid
until you found the "one"
across the street, around the corner and
14 stoops away.

Who could know or tell you
That you might find wise, whether it was
really love, this feeling you mostly
did not analyze that you often kept buried
deep inside, more offered to offspring than
her, still you thought it to be true and given

until the Broadway lights beckoned
sidewalks glistened, and a tune occupied your
mind, a symphony of choices of other needy,
lonely women, and whatever love was then
faded like your lousy poker hands, and you drew
cards forever, hoping to find a stand pat hand
and love was gone, and never seemed so far
away

until, it returned in one warm bed, for a few
nights, to get out of the damn sleet, and just
feel star struck, to spend a night, and drink coffee
before 6am, and talk about the back and forth of
a good life

and that lasted, feeling in love, all those days
and more children, committed for all time until the
forces would come and take them all away
loved them, then and still,
even after she said enough, "goodbye"

no surprise, love can't overcome
distance, silence, an interior life,
no time for anyone, no compassion, and
the routine of years together, same food,
same vacation spots, same movies, same clothes,
same side of the bed, it all gets very, very, old
ancient

even if you still have it, that feeling you cannot
set aside, that let you abide it all
perhaps she never really loved you after all
or did anyone else
more convention than enthralled
duty than connection
obligation than commitment
what is done, not what is felt

does it come and go
is it eternal for anyone
ethereal, chemical and
cognitive
intense only to fade like everything else
except our essence

not gone, perhaps but hibernating
awaiting the ensuing spark
it is off the list, for now,
a full night's sleep, a warm day,
a little less pain, and a hello from anyone
is enough to keep you going.

Until love returns…

Panel 16E- Line 94

A leap unexpected and miraculous
From an orphan home on Staten Island
Mount Loretto that housed him
brothers and sisters after mom got sick and
dad couldn't cope anymore

to his name
Angel Mendez on this black wall
Where a man he saved stands crying
on a winter night
he leans on crutches, adjusts his shoulder holster
and wipes his glasses
and remembers, what he cannot ever forget
not a nightmare, but a memory like a prayer
that occupies his mind, sometime most days

even when he was on the bench
of the Supreme Court of Pennsylvania
this man, once a platoon lieutenant in
Vietnam, Lt. Ron Castille
Will not let that one day go
in far away Duc Pho
16 March of '67

out to search and destroy
under heavy fire and he was
cut down, a leg gone, among other
life threatening blows
immovable, ready to go with honor
and quietly

Angel moves towards him
Firing all the way
Picks him up and drags him
75 meters to safety away
incoming hits his shoulder but he will
not relent

and could have stopped there
heroic for what he had done
but
decided to protect the rear as they
carried the Lt. away
fateful as such stories go
caught another round that ended
a young life,
2nd battalion, 7th Marine
KIA, on this day

Chief Justice Castille knows
An entire life would have faded away
had Angel not acted heroically that day
sure there have been accolades, medals,

plagues, schools named,all in some minor way
saluting sacrifice,humility, and what we used
to call bravery clearly on display

what can anyone say for such valor
under fire
except to place a hand over his name
on this wall, offer a prayer
and hope that you will never forget
and that he can hear you say
"thank you Angel, I wish you were here,
Love you.. man"

The Only Honest Writing

is what you write to yourself
not expecting anyone to read it but you
or upon review, you know
it's all auto-biography, every sentence
soaked in your point of view
characters pieces of you, disassembled
and soldered together to soothe the ripped
psyche that is essentially all you

what a release it would be
just to write, freely with
no one else in mind, but the
expression of self after solace that
only expressing it can bring
to only you, expecting nothing else
but the expulsion of any thought from the
inner citadel of stoic thoughts

Aurelius did it, or so it seems
scribed his thoughts over twenty years
and you would not gather from the smatterings of
a Roman mind expressed in Greek that he is more
than a man after improvement, not an emperor from

160 A.D.
Marcus after what we all seek
Knowing who we are, what we can become,
And how we hold onto our moral core
If there is one

Can you be kind and still be firm
Be generous, even to your enemies
Guided by a rational mind, even when
tempted by excesses of power, carnality,
and not yield to anger, jealousy, envy,
or greed?

And have the presence to write of it
with some utter intelligence as
the Antonine plague piled bodies on funeral
pyres
as the Macromannic Germans came across the
Danube, uninterested in your "Golden Age"

Honest speech, and right action
written to himself, knowing that the forces
would descend, and he like all else would fade
and be forgotten, his humility stronger than
his prescience

we are not Emperors
with no nation's burden of destiny to
watch over
quest for nothing more than a day without

infamy
to write a few words that are true
that have no consequence to anyone but
you

words that get you through another day
on the way to a destination from which
you have detoured before
afraid of what
you find there behind that old fig tree,
honesty............

A Walk in the Rain

Who knows when you awaken
from sleep, where you actually slept
most of the night, where the guys upstairs
stopped screaming at each other and their
girlfriends, and the Ukrainian gal finally stopped
talking on her phone on the balcony, and went
inside to do whatever she does to herself at 3 am

outside the only color is grey
gather enough quarters, for the w and d
before the tattoo couple from New Brunswick
bring the laundry for a regiment
do the carry water, chop wood,
Zen dance
wash and scrub all the porcelain
vacuum when it gets to be 8, so as not
to overly irritate the ingrate most recently
an inmate, one floor below

so I walk out into the mist leaning towards
rain
head north, agreeing with myself to not turn around
until it stops

sage and jasmine nudge at my olfactory
barely overtaking the vomit by the Mercedes Benes
most blocks have deposits of crap from those yappers
pulled along by strong legged, big hipped, hooded women
sandals left on grass, a tank top hanging from a tree,
the proverbial black panties under a car wheel,
spit over puddles, a single, soaked Sunday newspaper
that will not be read with coffee and bread
a 100% silk tie, purple and white, here now around a pole after
a hopefully celebratory night

a lawn adorned with discarded cereal boxes, red drinking cups
one white sox, the Racing Form, and a table where boys
play beer pong,toppled by a sofa, knifed to expose the foam
within

observing, nothing of note in my mind
expecting no revelation, seeking some solace
demanding purpose to reveal itself among the
flotsam of the streets
as I walk north waiting for the rain to end

Every 17 Years

They come from underground
buried for 17 years
red eyes peering through darkness
a legion of millions
casting a black cloud over every field below
incessant chirping, signaling their presence
only driven to stay above ground long
enough to mate, lay eggs and dive
back into the soil, only to emerge
decades later, again

Cicadas come
cast a frightening presence
mythology tied to locusts, which they are not
harmless mostly
but unseemly, gross, and
out of a Hitchcock scene
part of a distorted subplot

the boss told me to get my camera
and the cruiser and go check out
an infestation across the rice and soybean
fields in Paragould

at 2am
I drive into town, the only light across miles of
Pitch black fields, turn off the siren and the lights
Hear, crackles, as if I'm driving over a street of saltines
Turn on the headlights and see them everywhere
Below, on my windshield and cover the entire car

Encased in a blanket of them, all chirping away
I hit Jimmy Swains bar, and he yells to stay away
Enter anyway
The entire bar is walled with them, over mirror,
on the bar, on every wall, and the sound is high – fi
loud
I hear women screaming
finding two teens covered in cicadas
holding a flashlight, which once tossed
frees them

I take out my cameras, document the invasion
Set up lights to intensify the swarm
The boss is happy we calmed the folks down
Cruised the streets until dawn, as the horde
Receded, and the shop keepers came out to sweep up the
carcasses

harmless invasion
frightening no less
the snakes and lizards feasted

the hawks and crows too
a few good ole boys fried a few for chuckles
and I ate some, spit them out is my memory

sent the film to the Natural History Museum
in Paris, France who wanted it for their
records, I guess there are no cicadas over there
where grapes and wheat, replace soybeans and rice
the only infestation they get are bad ideas and immigrants
from everywhere
I'd rather drive through Paragould, in the middle of the night
hear the cicadas wail, and my tires crunch, every 17 years…

4 May

Phnom Penh
Nixon proclaimed was a place
we had to invade
not enough to be in Saigon, Hue,
the La Trang Valley, bombing the hell out of
the Ho Chi Minh trail, blasting away in Mai Lai
now it was off to another damn jungle with
hollow cheeked boys from Kalamazoo to
Kent, Ohio

That speech brought out the
Hippies, known malcontents with
the senseless war, a ragtag gaggle of
drifters, students, and really smart kids
who thought any protest was better than silence

trucks came too
with young fellows in khaki
and rifles they had never fired
there to show force, over what no one really
knew
aimed their rifles at the shouts, afraid more than
under some resolve to shut them up or down

one shot birthed 59 more
four dropped, their blood preceding them to the grass and
concrete
through the screams and sirens
a lone girl wailed
over Jeffery Miller, on her knees
hoping for sanity and safety

Opa- locka far away
Hitchhiked this 14 year old runaway
Smoked some pot, cut classes
So hated her life, took off in flight
searching, barefoot, sleeping in fields
finding this

not wanting to be this part of history
caught in a photograph by happenstance
by one John Filo
who saw her, snapped it
and tried to send it, but was rejected
until he pursued it, knowing he had
a picture for all time that was
raw, and told everything that ever needed to be
or could be said about that one moment in
time
when the divisions were so clear, and anger ruled
over reason, and everyone was afraid of each other
and most hated, any alternative point of view

Mary Ann Vecchio could not know
where her thumb would take her
how at 14, all the growing up she ever needed
would come in 45 seconds and 60 shots,in Ohio
on a day in May

mayday, mother's day, and national prayer day
all get recounted and remembered
not the 4 of May
to afraid we are, still, to see that photo in our
minds' eye, drift towards the memory,
see the blood, and terror in her face
and have the screams rattle us again
that all of that actually happened
here..

Accusations Everywhere

Does not matter who are
the swells gets the most
in a land where nothing is true
anyone can accuse you

recently men who want to be
one of the nine Supremes
sit in utter despair and a women
from somewhere in another time
says men of letters, law, and consequence
treated her in a foul way

told her filthy jokes
commented upon her dress
touched her in a unwanted place
invaded her private space
even dared to say he wanted her
in a carnal way

in halls once hallowed by the presence of
great men a woman from the college years
ask that he repent for holding her down
scaring her psyche on a frat party night

pressing his besotted, if clothed, body
against her in a way that presaged
rape was on the way

no matter if these accusations are ever
true
it is enough to use them
daggers to hearts
set on being of value in their time
to have it murdered in their prime
by the unwanted, unfounded
only to be declined, the accusers fade into
footnotes, and the blood wiped up by an orderly

and if you dare write of men who mishandled women
like Philip Roth, your books and publisher evaporate
with accusations from women of the past
who suddenly, now want their claims of rape to
last
entwined he is in such debate this Blake Bailey
fellow, who is well know
a biographer no less, years of work withdrawn
banished, if you will
and he is sent straight to hell
by one Valentina Rice, who with all her power
and acclaim, come snow to accuse him of a dastardly
act, done, and secret for years

where is Zola now
J'Accuse required to tame or demand

evidence, a presumption of innocence
perhaps, a full throated cry, that damned a nation
for railroading, Dreyfus, a convenient Jewish scapegoat

women walk with daggers in daylight
bringing accusations
unfounded, we cannot know
stabbing targets in the front, slicing
throats
so these men know, whatever, they did do
or not
will haunt them, and weaken them
as their blood flows into the gutter
of unproven accusations running off
into a river of doubt

A Cider Jar in a Beer Cooler

21 parts of cortex
cut into 240 blocks
in Wichita
hidden away, after she threw him
and Einstein's brain specimens out
of Dr. Thomas Harvey's proper
Princeton house

Doc lost his job
Drove from town to town
With Einstein's brain parts in his trunk
Believing that smart guys would find
a revelation, in these dried out cells,
of how their owner could conjure
relativity, space time, field theory
all in what appeared to be, a normal sized
and constructed brain

as the century turned, phrenology was in
play
smart guys lined up when dead
to give their brain away after their
demise

to "brain clubs" of the day
popped them out, let them dry
sawed away, to see if they could see
what made this bloke extraordinary

A lab boy had Walt Whitman's
in a large jar
slipped through his hands
splattered on a clean floor
thought to pick it up and start again
but finally relented
Whitman's head was large, brain not as much
No one thought they would find anything
substantial

Mc Kinley's assassin
Leon Czolgosz was electrocuted just a
month after he shot him dead for
the working man he said
before his body turned cold, they sawed open
his skull, put the brain on a plate
and waited for it to cool
found nothing they could
before DNA, electron microscopes
and super computers
just a regular brain that decided
one day in March in Buffalo to
remove William for Teddy

and there maybe something to it

a larger pre frontal cortex here
a parietal lobe bulges there
a thicker medulla oblongata
motor cortices larger in one hemisphere
than the other
an anatomic clue to genius, or what makes
one man do the incredible or the insane
you can sit at your dandy computer and
see the difference of a schizophrenic brain
the creeping growth of beta amyloid plaque
so you can see disease for sure but beyond that
not much more

Dr. Harvey lasted longer than Einstein
No one wanted to slice up his brain at 94
All the cider jars were gone, anyway

The Orange Sun Sinks

Just below the marine layer returning
now
a damp grey blanket signaling
retreat from the turquoise surf
the sun's orange light bathes the
sea from horizon half way to shore

and I stop and take it in even as tears
well, not for the beauty of the landscape
but for all the sunsets seen with someone
in love, you imagined, unrequited
only to find then and there or years after
was a lie
so I wipe my face

the lifeguards yell at the suited surfers
"come on in, now ",
"see you guys at first light"
With an admonition
"if anything goes wrong after I'm gone
Call 911, dudes"

A tall young women, with hair, unfurled to

Mid- back is sweetly agitated, and tightens thonged
Butt
"Let's go already, Danny, I'm cold
Let's go dammit"

Lighter fluid smell overtakes
all the marijuana aromas
mellow mood turns to rising orange
flames, as pallets ignite, in bonfires
of nightfall delight
all huddled under blankets
a virtual ad hoc tribe of true believers
in the elevated life of surf and sand
awash in tones of grey and black
fires flame
it is quiet, a moment
I run between two million dollar house
find a dark space and squat like a Tanzanian
hunter/gatherer, and crap for the first time in
a week, as if, I'm a Hadza tribesman
bury it, straighten up,
limp out and inhale the jasmine, and sage
and mark it up as one damn good day

Nazi's of a Different Hue

They are everywhere
Nazi's
What Adolph wrought
Thought burned in a bunker in '45
After his deserved demise
Million murdered, more dead in battle
Rubble everywhere
But the nihilist philosophy always there

Essentially a code of hate
Anyone not like me
Not for what they believe or say
But just who they are, that cannot be altered
You are always a Jew, Polish, Slavic, or worse a
Russian
Nothing you can ever do to elevate you
The Nazi will let you know you are under them
Untermenschen

The old neo Nazi's are almost quaint
Klan, Southern racists, Jew and black hating gangs
A few left overs with Swastika flags on rec room walls
A framed picture of Lincoln Rockwell, over a bedside table

Where Mein Kampf lays translated, unopened

No need to be a fake Aryan race
or have blonde hair, sky blue eyes
the Chicago river runs black
Lori Lightfoot by name, Mayor of Chicago
Into some bizarre Hall of Shame
refuses to be interviewed by whites
only people of color now
an "equity lens" tells her
only blacks and browns need
stay- all you white folks go on your way

Nazi's for Palestine
Always been that way, even back in Hitler's day
Burly men roaming Beverly Hills
Asking folks, dining, "Are you a Jew"?
Slashing, beating, spraying them
But that's ok
Because Israel belongs only to them
Time to wipe the Jew scum away

No yarmulke 's in West LA
No stars of David around your neck
A walk to synagogue may end with you
Running for your life, pursued by pickup trucks
of Palestinian men screaming
"get the fuckin Jew"

There are Nazi's in the streets

All of a different hue
Expanded their hate to include more than
Only the diminishing population of Jews
Old and white, anyone who dislikes exclusion
Entitlement of one race over another
You all are targets too
First you declare you are harmed
Ask for reparations
Take whatever you wish
Loot, topple, terrorize
Exclude who you despise, scapegoat the best you can
Marginalize anyone who is not like you
And then demand, compliance or else
Anyone ready for a Sieg Hiel?

Where Has My Libido Gone?

I had one
Most men do
It comes with hormones
flowing through you, testosterone overtaking
Sense and thought
Raging for attention, turning days
into crusades for conquest
devising strategic plots to land
on and within someone

daydreams of insertions
prompting wood rising under
classroom desks
fumbling through dating
unhooking bras,wrangling girdles
begging for a buddies Buick back seat
to round the bases
after weeks of foreplay
and meeting her parents

And I thought it might go away
after the regularity of marriage
sending sperm to egg a few times

did not subside, no ebb and flow
just rose again, from time to time
secretaries, maids, check out gals, and
society types,
all, alluring
intensive enough to
bring it across the blood/ brain barrier, you should know
better

probably still there
deeply sunk into the domain of
what men used to do
different now
can appreciate beauty, and sexuality
but no lights flash, no sirens wail
no drive to follow her anywhere
content to reflect what it might be like to
indulge a single night, too far to go for
a few moments of friction anyway

but it would be nice, even with the libido locked away
to hear a woman say, "that was really nice, Joe"

Weary of Rebuke

Critics proliferate
Multiply electronically,
Mouths without brains proclaiming
Points of view, derived from fragments
Of truth, populating cyberspace
Banshees with thumbs in a frenzy of
Emotion
Passionate, obstinate spews spitting
Rebuke upon you
If you
Dare

Disagree or just not care
After you, eternally, feeding upon your
Despair
Labeled you become, what they want you to become
obliterated by the army of anonymous
zombies
desiccated, soulless, hulks
rotted by hate and singular view
silently screaming night and day
that what you think must be crushed
every single day

unable to understand
we are all not universally interested
in everything
they may care about whales, icebergs,
where monarch butterflies go in winter
faceless protein, exterminating steers and cows
banning sugar, taxing your commute by the mile,
reading children books about drag queens, never saying
him or her, they or them
whatever

and if you venture onto less tangible ground
of thought, meaning, or even purpose you
are lynched for noble thought by the purveyors of
critical review

why is it bold to stand for
freedom, equal opportunity, liberty
without restraint, tempered by responsibility
a kind heart and belief in God or at least something
bigger and universal in us all
do that and be impaled, burned with
wet wool blankets on your chest
hung with piano wire by the all knowing
unseen, unnamed, electronic mob
you only have the right to say what they
believe, an orthodoxy of the scum and slime
bathing you in the gutter run off of modern
times

weary of all rebuke
worn by criticism
tired of smashing zombie heads
filled with the same positions
on everything you disagree
the plight of opinion and opposition
to just be quiet now
yield to virtual bullets and remain upset

not likely
man the barricades!

Photos in an Arcade Booth

Almost ran over them
next to the roller coaster
A strip of photos from an arcade
photo booth, the one with a curtain
where you could cram you and all your
buddies inside, mug and clown until
the flash
and that was that, a piece of what you are and
were, on a dozen exposures, you could fold
up and jam into your wallet
or even toss away, like this one
In a puddle starring at those who pass
Almost covered by the cotton candy stem
With its pink residue floating over three
tan faces
with world healing smiles

inside with the curtain closed
adolescent worries, a litany of
fears, shut away,
purity coming in the space between
the coins falling and that flash
confirming you were here that day

with a goofy smile
a tongue wagging
the obligatory two fingers behind
an unsuspecting head
a toothy grin, eyes wide open
even a kiss on lips you may never
touch again or be near your cheek
for all time

outside the surf rises
rides twirl and frighten
children scream, delighted
popcorn and hot dog aromas
overtake the grey waifs of MJ
exhaled by the drummer behind the
bandstand

arm in arm
clusters of friends, with pictures
in their pockets
walk through neon, bathed in red and yellow
light, care free
untouched by whatever is their reality
not concerned by what is next, to come
or any design or destiny

I wish I had those pictures
taken by the shore
of friends, and loves that might
last forever

eyes seeing a better life, bitterness
unrevealed, sorrow and loss yet to
appear
the buoyancy of youth
the bravado caught in a flash
that feeling that when I pulled
back the curtain
it would all somehow last…

Cowboys and Country Music

Can't be a cowboy anymore
They want the Ryman closed
Love songs, unrequited, adventures from
farm to fields, standing by your man,
Sleeping single in a double bed,
Living in a place where you won't be
fenced in, under starry skies above
exchanged for bumps and grinds
porno on display, ass grinding movements,
lyrics about the in and out, celebrating
fluid exchanges or
men playing gangsta at night

we need more Patsy Cline, Tammy,
Dolly, Coal Miner's Daughters', Cash,
And Strait
Poets of music you could relate
Simple folks after common things
Laying line for the county
Building cars for Fords
Fighting for the gal you love
Leaving your exes in Texas
Having friends in low places

Just being an Okie from Muskogee

Haggard at full voice
Willie with his pigtails
Kris coaxing us
"to just make it through the night"
Cash lighting the ring of fire
Inside us all
Most of that gone and vilified
To be country pushed aside, as if it was
Some defiled philosophy, opposed
To the current rants and chants
of equity, systemic racism, and
reparations rants

where did equal opportunity go
rugged individualism, a horse and saddle life
six guns, campfires, roundups, and campin'
out of your truck
is it all gone now, if the new elite have any luck

its time to bring back Roy and Dale
Autry, Loretta, Hank, Waylon, circle the wagons
with the current of country's best,
so no one can forget, it's our America too
the once revered red, white, and blue

more cowboy and country
can bring us all back to reason
more that unites us than not

not a diminished view at all
unless we let it be withered
by the pompous few who hate everything we do
hard working, God fearing, folks who never asked
for anything more than their freedom
to pursue whatever happiness might be out there
for me and for you
and a chance to play on any given day
"I'm proud to be an American"
And mean it.....

Mercury in Retrograde

The forces align in malevolent ways
sometimes and you know
to lay low so
the forces cannot find you
but they do, anyway

the full moon, dubbed Flower
awaits its eclipse at 4am
bone weary, you still rise to see it
behind low clouds
two girls on a balcony snap their
phones, in a hugging self portrait
to join the multitude of less celestial
images as they document otherwise
unremarkable lives

I rise, run, shave
Can't find the car, search the old man's search
expecting I left it, in a forgotten place
gone, stolen or towed
towed, by a predatory Mad Max
dude before or after, probably after
the eclipse

sticker and license didn't jibe
the peril of the average man
refusing to read instructions that
are not difficult deductions
rage rises as I call to find the damn
car, and download, enough angst based
crap to bury a AAA convention, to a poor
guy named Assad

"it's not me man, they told me to tow you"
"250 and its yours, miss a day another 75"

You get the mass shooter
Upset with his boss, and years of
loss, isolation, faces pained to talk to you,
becomes obsessed with revenge
burns his house, packs his pockets with ammo
and blows away ten people
and quiets himself, as
Mercury is in retrograde

The car keepers at Expedite Towing
wear Glock's
eat enormous Number #1
In and Out burgers
And are unhappy to interrupted
Mid bite
I put aside the outrage, misplaced anger,
And become a compliant, suck up to
get the car

finally riding the wave of the forces
glad I left the shotgun in the closet
and the :38 in the bedside table

open the windows
all of them
head towards the beach
devoted to talking to no one
turn off the devices and hope
it is over for this cycle
and the forces will move on
leave me alone, neither forward nor reverse
some sublime homeostasis
just let me sit on this concrete bench
watch the sun kiss the horizon and hear the
sea birds swoon…

Neither Aaron nor Rose

Waiting for talent to appear
Can take more than a few years
If it ever does show it itself
There are prodigies of math,
song, violin
Mozart types, prolific SOB's,
Not limited savants, but genetically
designed to soar through societal norms
to be obviously gifted, in what it is they
do, and contribute to

Ruth and DiMaggio
Williams, The Black Bomber,
Ali, Lebron and Chamberlin
Lenny Bernstein, Yoyo Ma,
Satchmo, Ella and the Duke
Elvis, or Chuck Berry
Thorpe, Phelps, even Bruce
Jenner

Talent they could not contain
abstain, compartmentalize or delay
from its presence to startle and enthrall

the rest of us all
attempting to explain to ourselves what
talents might dwell, yet, to be displayed
before our old age

I thought I'd get to 715
Like Hank, break a record of note
Have a name in some accounting that I was
here, and mattered for a moment
until the next talented dude emerged

time walks past you on the road to Damascus
on your way to find out what you have to offer
besides just getting on with it
life that is, until talent outs itself, as weariness
sets in, I get that there is no 715 ahead
but, to be Pete instead
just keep showing up, like Cobb, for every
game
and playing it as if it was both first and last

I wonder if that is a talent of some measure
to get up
shower and shave
walk across the razor's edge
earn a buck, pay the bills, manage a smile or two,
offer whatever it is that stands for love,
to a selected few
get the kids through school, hold onto what seems true
and stay away from what paralyzes you

talent or not
that's all I got
not Aaron or Rose
no records of note just
showing up for life, day to day
extracting some meaning, perhaps,
more absorbing the blows and ducking
the right crosses
and showing up for the later rounds....

Fruit Mix in Extra Light Syrup

I would like to be lighter of heart
and spirit, less engaged with interior
thoughts at this stage, deep into ACT lll
not knowing if an ACT IV is even there

Buoyant, carefree, except for the morning ache
In a known place or metastasized somewhere
To bother me throughout the day, only to be replaced
By a chronic toothache, knotted gut, or muscle spasm
Searching for that oasis, across a desert of pain and worry
to sip, to be pain free
and to pause, reflect that its ok, still to be above ground
worth the toil, to be above the soil

I find a bag of canned foods
Left by the mailboxes by a departing
tattooed would be middle weight contender
no cameras to catch me rummage
select a few, and be on my way
only to discover I have no opener
for these cans of fruit in syrup

I unsheathe that aged US Army bayonet

my father's, US M3 Camillus, still encrusted with Burma
mud from the Irrawaddy, in '44
knife it open
pour it into a black plastic bowl
and sit by the window, listening to the
motorcycles rev, across the midnight road

serenity invades me
light syrup and cut fruit brightens the
darkness within
slow walking each spoon of it
reflecting upon nothing
purity from a discarded can
accomplishing nothing more than
this moment of bliss

Hilary and Norgay knocked off
Everest this day
Weiner Heisenberg at Heigoland
conquered particle physics, gazing over the
North Sea, and I,
opened a can of mixed fruit in light syrup,
and thought it transcendent, perhaps I have lost my mind…

Henry Ford Rolling in the Grave

A farm boy born during the Civil War
school drop out
figured a way to let us all drive
today
car for every workingman, that he could
take wherever he wanted, any Goddam day
made it the American way, and Ike
went about creating the highways

now the global warming yahoos want
to take it all away
especially in that California welfare state
where to save 1% of CO2 emission for the planet
they want to eradicate the engine and fuel
that got us here, so they can save
us all from rising seas, melting glaciers,
and the like

so, they want to force us all into electric cars
even if there are 500,000 recharge stations still
undone
and then tax anyone who has one, for how many miles
you drive

to make up for the gasoline tax they will destroy
of their own insane creation
and still pay folks who own trees to not cut them for
lumber for all those affordable homes we need
so their buddies can collect cap and trade fees
and make out fine, as we attempt to pay for
the EV's, the solar batteries, and the extra electric
fees

just between you and me, its all a con

the oligarchs get to own a car
you get to ride a rail
live in a cluster near a transport hub
designed by them to control you
forced to take a train
because they took your tax money and built
a half a trillion dollar network of rail and
such, just so the "underserved" can get to work

first they take your truck
then your wife's sedan
tax you for energy, and more when its in high demand
get rid of nuclear energy
put floating windmills offshore
create fields of solar batteries
put you on the grid so they
can black you out if you don't agree
keep the power on for those who do
laugh as you cram yourself into a trolley,

wait for a bus, or lose your mind as your daughter
gets stabbed for a few bucks texting her mother
on the way to school on a high speed train to
oblivion

Old timers used to say
"bet he's rolling in his grave"
Expect ole' Henry Ford is now
a few miles from where he was born,
sent Ford's down an assembly line
and changed a nation's style

and now the smart asses will eradicate it all
to make the air cleaner, and the world greener
you buyin' that?

There is a Fear

That most men have
If they own up to it
palpable, nightmarish
plausible not obtuse
eyes open at 3am
sweat across your chest
getting up to change a t-shirt
turn on all the lights, sit on the sofa
stare at an enormous blank television screen, you just bought
to watch the NFL
and you hug yourself to
hold back your screams

not of heights, leaping from planes,
root canals, snakes and spiders, roaches
across bedroom rugs at night
whether our wife has the Braca
gene, your kids will go to hell
or even fail at earning to spell

just that you are out of work
money running low
you've knocked on all those

proverbial doors, once open
now closed
names crossed off lists
no one returns the calls
you sit at the kitchen table
searching for some unturned stone
head in hands
anguished, tearless
determined but momentarily defeated

phone rings
and you calculate is it that guy who will
redeem you or is it the collectors voice
soft spoken threats ending your swipe
and buy
everything on hold, the focus of a man
with his neck in Judge Roy Bean's noose
in one of the late night you have on to
pass time during insomniac hours

stand at a pump, 3.60 in your pocket
two gallons worth to get you to the next
interrogator
and your hand is cold in March
watching the numbers roll, you
dare not let it flow, but squeeze it out
money will be gone by fall
and you cannot conjure begging your
father in law

two kids, a wife,
no prospects
in a March rain
rather be back in a warm jungle
stalking bad guys through ear high
elephant grass

One August Day Outside Mexico City

The days of well known men
once celebrated, venerated
or
feared and hated
revert to patterns after a while
mundane
even as revenge cannot be contained
furors calmed, or scores unsettled
compel action that is frustrated once
out of power and range

tending to cactus in his yard
in a leafy neighborhood
feeding rabbits who became his pets
and diversion
from a life of demanding change
railing against monarchy, anarchy,
even Communism, in the hands of a
a tyrant, who only wanted him dead

Trotsky knew as he sat at his table
writing polemics still, hoping to carry
weight against Stalin, from this exile place

that this would be his
final home, and last revolutionary act
many attempts over years
white Russians, soldiers, rivals,
always found him, and failed

two trips to Siberia
banished to Turkey on to
France, but, not Paris
watched as if he as headed on a train
like Lenin to start it all again
asked around, and found Mexico
would let him in, as the Nazi's fooled
Chamberlin
Old Joe called for show trials
And convicted Leon, in absentia
Murdered all the rest
He knew he was next

Rivera let him stay with him and Frida
until he laid her, a few nights in a row
all white hair, and pointed beard still had
appeal it seemed to artists who loved
his schemes
come they did, shot his grandson in the foot
chased away by students who were his bodyguards
most days
and he laughed and fed the rabbits the next day

had a .35 by his side that August day
Ramon took out an ice axe, the adze edge
cracked his skull, cut his brain, blood
across the floor
he watches as they almost beat Ramon to death
until Trotsky asks them to relent before he
finally collapses on the floor

only fearsome to the deranged
a revolutionary without a following
a man stateless, until Mexico took him in
on the lame from his destiny
until it caught up to him
at the blunt end of an iceaxe..

Admonitions

Never cease until you're gone
always a mouth open somewhere
telling you what to do
watch out for
avoid, review, contemplate
a danger that they see
an experience to save you from
spewing at you, as though you
are just plain dumb

a litany of don'ts
overwhelming the to do's
a barrage of sputtered taunts of
exactly what not to do

Every admonishment with a consequence
unspoken yet known
if you touch that you'll get burned
eat that slowly please
milk and meat will make you ill
you better learn to swallow that large pill
put this on before you go out
you'll need gloves, and boots

if you start smoking now, you'll die young
that's not the type of girl you should date
turn off the damn TV, get your homework done
you better learn to fight now
if you would just speak up- you'd be alright
don't stay out with her all night

you get a ticket speeding, the car keys are gone
leave the radio alone
is it really love or are you just horny
don't get married before you land that job
better save some cash for later, you have kids now

can't you just listen to me
Stop yelling a me over every thing
you need to spend some time with them
Don't forget your parents' anniversary
All this hard work is getting us nowhere
You better have a B plan

And on it goes
Stay within the lane
Watch out for those outliers
If you don't vote this way, there is hell to pay
Better buy an EV now, your Mustang is too old to ride anyway

keep your mouth shut, no one cares
what you have to say
stay invisible, it is safer

stop writing that crap, it's a useless display
be content to have nothing
it's ok to be ascetic, require not much
and get totally out of touch
with who you are
thought you might be
would you have been derailed, if not a
single admonition came your way
would the world still spin without
the vocal direction, pretending to seek
perfection
wondering why you never heard the furies say
"find your own way"

Batting Cage

They were not there when a boy
to face, a big green box with a conveyor belt
that spit out hardballs, consistently at
70 mph
With precision at an imaged strike zone
And you could hit all night, as long as the tokens
Held out
No Manny or Reds or Brew to throw
directly at you, under a dim light, less
engaged in your swing than their power
to tower over you, frightened into tentative
swings, afraid of the corners, and wondering, if
just for fun, they'd throw a curve at you, destined
for your cheek

that you ever learned to hit
settled in and slowed down Manny's fast ball
eyed Reds, knuckler, and eventually figured out
Brew's curve, testament enough to that higher
power, a pinch of innate ability, but mostly
grit

Williams, Aaron, Ashburn,
Joe D, Mantle, Maris, Mays
Bonds, Clemente, Reggie
To name a few
All in your mind as you'd swing
And hit some long and clean
The bat vibrating in young hands
The sound of the sweet spot roams
Inside your head,yet, today

Children grown and gone
Alone with no one to take there
Only one in a cage with pure white hair
poised in muscle memory to face the
machine, and pretend you can hit a fastball
once again
too old to fear it
waiting for it, slapping
a few barely
until a rhythm returns
coaxing a natural swing without a pang
of pain knocking four in a row
feeling 18, the best twenty bucks spent
in a damn, mostly depressing year…..

Last of the Liberators

He had rolled his T-34 tank treads
over the dead, from Stalingrad and
Kursk to this place
He had shrapnel tear a way his own flesh
Three times, always returning to his duty
and his men, and this tank

fighting for Mother Russia was neither
nightmare nor dream
just what young, David Dushman was called
to do, fight with the Red Army and
annihilate Hitler, and give the Nazi's
their due
crush them under his machine without
remorse or cheers
just do it and dream of better years

he pulled to stop
saw an electric wired fence
around the place, his commander called
Auschwitz
Flattened it that January Day

Not knowing at first what he would see
Skeletons in piles, with thin paper thin
Falling out the barracks, so weak to sit on the
dead, and he threw food cans at them
barely paused as they chased their tormentors
into the woods

he could not know
a million souls murdered inside
that flattened fence
and now he is gone at 98, the last
Soviet soldier who saw it raw

Did his job
Fought for the cause and
Like others,moved on
Even as Stalin purged his father
Shattered the communist promise
of a new,modern,Russia

he fenced, coached Olympians
was at Munich when Black September
slaughtered Israeli athletes
he had only a foil and not his tank
but memories of the death camp
never were far away
few men become legendary
less twice

a liberator, and a world class coach
fitting legacy, of note
to a young man who drove his T-34
into a piece of history, that had to be remembered, never
forgotten, nor would he ever let it be....

Last Night in Rancho Mirage

A deeply tanned face stares into a mirror
flashes a rack of bright white caps smile
rubs a towel cross a mostly bald head
pulls his collar up, as he has done a
thousand times,
cleaning up after making fresh sausage,
ready to visit his gal, before his birthday
the next day

Ermenigildo knows it's a long way from the
streets of New York City to here
where he drives down Dinah Shore Drive
drops off cleaning on Bob Hope
turns right on Dean Martin, and winds his way
to Sinatra drive

He knows how he got here
from his place, Jilly's at 52nd and 8th
he and Frank were sympatico from the
gitgo, two kids from the street with
different skills

Jilly did it all for Frank
Driver, valet, bodyguard,
Advance man, mostly confidant
Even best friend,
if the Chairman really had any
by the time he was 74, about to turn
another year
it was over 30 years together
and he looked unfazed, unworn
appeared robust, fully alive and ready
finally for the salad years
whatever the hell that meant
he would say

sure he looked mobbed up but wasn't
when he turned the key to his car that
night to go see his girl, the car didn't blow
up, whatever drama there might have been
evaporated over the years in the desert
heat
even that wrap over securities fraud
turned into probation, and community service
nothing more

so his head was clear
Jilly turns the white Jag onto Gerald Ford Drive
And a 29 year old, who just gulped three beers at
Don Diego's
slammed into him
Jeffery Perrotte, a serial lush, saw the car in flames

ran over, heard Jilly scream, then just left the scene
Jilly suffocated, and burned
a few minutes after twelve on what would be his
75th birthday

A New York kid who got to be somebody
hobnobbed with the big shots, stood by the
Great one, and when Frank died, buried in the same
cemetery plot, 600 came to say sayonara, and Sinatra
carried the casket
when he died, he was interred, six plots away
Frank with his Jack Daniels, cigarettes, a lighter
and a roll of dimes so he could call his buddies from
beyond
Jilly with his memories, the big smile, and awaiting the call
from the Boss……
Jeffery went away for 23 years, finally paroled, after finally
telling the board, he was sorry for what he did on, Jilly's last night in
Rancho Mirage

Going 80 on a Desert Road

When everything hurts
pre- arthritic neck only turns right,
barely left
pulled rectus muscle from pretending to be
Arnold
Unreliable bowels rebel
constantly
Mind cluttered with daydreams of poverty
exhaustion, no prospects whenever, whatever
this is
ends
insanity creeping into every neural pass

text in sick, who calls anymore
call Gary, working in clay on a statue he'll
install in Alaska, come Fall
"come on up, have a beer, it's 118, today"

Tune out O' Leary insisted
So you could hear the inside
Sit still, let your mind go
Let the thoughts emerge and fade
Hook onto none of them

Let go, shut it all off and drift
There is more in nothingness and a meditative
vacation from the to and fro
you require a mind enema, now and again

when I get to sea level
I turn off the air, doff the shades
No radio, no phone, nada
Heat comes from 76 to 112
And my mind travels everywhere
desperate to capture my consciousness
as I fight it off

the thoughts come
bizarre and mundane
dating Raquel Welch whose 80
being the last man in…
solo rowing the Pacific
sending the Reparations Committee
my thoughts
fasting for 26 hours, and how good I feel
pledging to sipping not gulping
eating slowly and less
was I capable of being a better father
regretting not serving in Vietnam
letting the beard and hair go
retiring to a desert hut, and write and
paint
being perceived as a lunatic, nut

sarcasm not a substitute for fame
losing the only woman,
I ever loved

Smells of fertilizer, cow dung,
Linger in my nostrils
Fields of grain, green and tan
Orange dust clouds, slow me down
from farmers in CAT hats
Inside air- conditioned cabs
working, at a job that has a start and finish
each day, observable accomplishment
not the ethereal, electron laden
pulses of my days

80 mostly
Stopping to change a shirt
Run water through my hair
And gas up,just east of Roll, AZ.
One long moving Zen, not wanting it
to ever end
sweat, a road, dust, and no one to confront
direct, or command,
critique free, momentarily
desert Nirvana…

Al is Not Al Anymore

Alan came from the same crowded street
64 houses on one side in a row
64 on the other
Hyman – Korman built them after the war
7500 bucks, a 90% loan guarantee, and a G.I. Bill
to go to school or work
Al played hard in the games between the curbs
20 feet across

Stick ball
Half ball, he hits 123 home runs one summer
Step ball, throwing it against a stoop
for bases earned
touch football, where his braces left a
life long scar above my wrist, as I tried to
block him to no avail
played varsity
had letters and pins all over his
black and red sweater
a jock, a handsome womanizer

no cash for college
butchered with his uncle Chas until

he decided to adventure in "the great Nam"
he would say
when he came back unscathed
except for a cracked front tooth and a lip scar
from flying shrapnel

took over the shop
raised three
stayed married to his high school flame
suffered through the in law game
survived it all with a cleaver, a bloody apron
and that handsome square jaw

prostate cancer came
the gave him drugs, over did it apparently
offset his hormone flow, knocked his
testosterone to hell
flushed him with estrogen
and he started to think, look like,
and want to become a women

maybe it was always Al inside
just a desire and compulsion he
figured he would hide
whether drugs or plain desire
he told me the other night
he is going to transition before
Labor day

And I said

"I don't care Al, I love you, man
either way"
and hope the rest of his world will
embrace him the same
and will be as blessed as I am to have
him as friend, whether Al or Alice
that will never end ....

Ultimate Cancel Culture Revenge

The blade came down 17, 000 times
revenge delivered to monarchs
named Louie and Marie
scientists and scholars too
Antoine Lavoisier and his wife to name two
And then even Robespierre
Heads in baskets for the same crime
Not agreeing with the new revolutionary state

The guillotine deployed seen by the august
through an "equity lens" so commoner and king
had the same "humane" fate
the idiocy of the of the rebellious, the injustice in the
sentence not the difference of gallows or blade

They came in crowds at first to cheer
The end of the prior ancien' regime
A culture change, canceling for certain the opposed
Knitting shawls and laughing at each demise
Until it went on, and they all knew it could be their
neck

Cancel it all, they now say
Can the guillotine be that far away?
no need for Fitzgerald and Sarah Vaughn
Johnny Mathis, Rawls, or even Nat King Cole
Rather deify ex whores, video pornographers
Violence peddling rappers
Fill the streets with peaceful protesters as fronts for
looters, shooters, whose anger surges, for wrongs
of past, as excuses for revenge and retaliation

Can it be that all of it is debased by
The premise of systemic race
If a culture changes the Gestalt where the background of
Hate emerges to obviate reform, progress, consideration
And actual contemplation, of how we are more the same
Even most noble causes can construct an edifice where terror reigns

No need for gallows, just sharpen the blade,
enough heads to roll,
until sanity returns

Grey Morning

For the crow on a perilous branch,
outside the window, dawn comes
grey,as it cackles to its compadres
one eye opens, barely to observe another
morning better to avoid than to stir
playing mind games, to commit to the singular
act of putting one foot on the floor
and doing so catapult my being into
beginning
Nunc Coepi say monastery priests who
have purpose imbedded from the Lord

No celestial guidance here
Excuses abound, to stay bound
to this nano- space, clean a toilet bowl,
dust everything, turn on the vacuum, cover
470 square feet, sweep the cobwebs with
an aged broom, sing quietly out of tune
seeking no one and nothing, allowing the grey
gloom to dictate what you do, putting away
ambition, tabling that ultimate search for meaning

a flicker of initiative ignites the smoldering fire
of activity, poking me out to plod a familiar path,
towards a shoreline, where the grey begins to dissolve
to a rising sun
steps become strides
sweat emerges
grace with gratitude come to an awakening mind
prayers too, for just being who I am alive
and not the other guy, pulling his face out of the sand
bed he occupied last night or the fellow shouting at a
gull, conversing with his demons
Ending it back at a pool
squeezing push ups
as two mallards walk by my nose
a matched pair, who doddle into the chlorine
I hear a splash, and turn to see a broad shouldered
older gal, named Maureen, getting ready for her laps
"how's it going?"
"pretty grey", I say
"it's always sunny to me ", she says convincingly,
And she swims with a perfect Australian crawl
on her way to 30 laps
The ducks paddle to the other end of the pool
And I'm glad I got that one foot out of the bed, on this grey morning

Tools

Worthless
Dumb
Under her control
Taken over by others
Devoid of your own perspective
Unable to find direction
Loss all independent selection
Manipulated by the world
Unable to break free
Live life on your damn knees
Silent when you need to speak
Fail to act independently
Pathetic, powerless
Ill defined
Capitulated to another power
That's over you
Afraid to veer away
Paralyzed to say your mind
Given up
Surrendering your free will
For some other time

It hurts, bringing anguished retaliation
when an adversary claims
you are a tool for saying or advising what
they cannot
knowing we all are, beholding, for cash,
job, family,fealty to a perceived benefactor,
higher power, who has something over us
long abandoned "free will" for survival
not cosmic to be sure, just the getting through
the days and nights
paying the bills
getting the kids through school
cancer treatments
stopping dental pain
having something to eat,
gasoline, a room to rent where the
schizophrenics that surround you don't come for you
because they know, you are unstable and
have guns

don't swing at the bastard that calls you
a tool
its not the school yard, or the alley behind
the Kosher butcher store, where you broke
Red's nose, and bit off half his left ear
For calling you a stupid asshole

Only academic retorts, now
Flourishes of rhetoric…

"you're such a tool"
"I am, I agree, but I'm a sharp knife, and you're a dull
butter knife, worn down by a pompous wife and her
socialist ideology"
And the tormentor pauses offering only
"you re an asshole, and they use you everyday"
And leaves for his echo chamber on the Hill

We are all tools sharp or dull
Attempting to delay our passage into hell
Find me the independent soul, who is not encumbered
Who speaks his actual mind, walks straight towards his
original point of view, and I'll become his tool too....

Don't Mess with the Gestalt

It is not static
What is background, unnoticed
foreground examined ad infinitum
Mutable, fixed until it's not
movement back and forth by natural forces
accelerated by human intrusion at everyone's
Peril
Once unexamined, or seen, pursued, reviewed
And pushed back out of view,
Only to be pulled into prominence again
And upset natural forces once calmed
To boil emotions once again

Regurgitated, to support a current point of view
out of the shadows in full measure revealing
unresolved enigmas, to complex or frightening
to conclude, hidden, for full measure to let us not focus
on this thing long past

poverty is there in the darkness, slavery, racism,
blacks killing blacks, drugs of all kinds, old brews and new
cocaine, heroin, and fentanyl too
a frozen legislative system, systemic sores, punks beating

Asians, each other, the weak, and of course, hating all the
Jews

Be careful what is in the background and what you pull forward
changing the Gestalt
Once on center stage, a solution not in view, can alter the trajectory
Of just what the hell we all do
Changing the balance, alters more than just the vibe
Riots come, the radicals vent, no one gives up anything
not even for Lent
And when the fires, end, what has been purified
other than a Malthusian venting
Step forward from the darkness, not just to give it light
but solve the damn problem or suffer it being in the spotlight

I can handle my Gestalt- where I notice skinny gals
walking great Danes and Newfoundlanders that I never saw before
or noticing chicken sandwich billboards, everywhere

Aloha shirts on old men, and Daisy Dukes revealing buttocks
on the girls in Little Italy
I can handle what I didn't see, but the other stuff
frightens the hell out of me…… They still managed to stay

The Turandot Three

Puccini thought it right
to have Turandot ask three questions
of her suitors
to add to the tragic drama of it all
get one wrong in this operatic quiz show
and your head would be sliced away
no one made it, until Act lll

questions for the opera and life are
mostly the same, riddles critiques might say
enigmas inside puzzles, if you remember the Balkans
by name
but, all with answers, unlike Zen koans
and by sword or other blade, you lose your head anyway
unresolved

for the Princess asked with elegant, mean- spirited class
what is born each night and dies at dawn?
Hope
What flares like flame, but is not?
Blood
What is the ice that gives you fire"
You, Turandot, says Calaf the mystery man

Famously off he goes, to a sleepless night and
opines, in a glorious tenor aria
Nessun Dorma, hoping she will not know
his name come morning
the last question to Puccini to save his thick neck
was
my name is Love….

And what of you four questions?

Who am I?
What is my purpose?
For what am I grateful?

Answer all of those, before you pretend know
What ACT you are in, what the outcome might be,
Or are you content to just let it all befall you as
It will, unanswered, unrevealed or examined out
Of what primal fear of knowing who you are
Being afraid of yourself, one step away from who
You really are

And the final question will still remain
If you dare to place before you, and give
You endless sleepless nights
Has any of this made you happy, even for a nanosecond?
or did you just take that off your list, knowing the life
you were leading will be amiss

Can you summon, the courage to leave your
Habit and life's cocoon, to renounce a life where
Questions are not asked, nor answered
And cry into the night that you will overcome
No matter what
Vincero!

Anger Comes

Everywhere there are outburst of
It
Fingers pointed, pushed into chests,
Mostly elevated voices, guttural incantations
Protean strings of expletives spewed
uncensored, never deleted
often of incident, momentary outrages
over parking spaces, line busters, not being
listened to
avoided, shunned, shamed
a wave of it ensues over you
anger, always the beats within
overtakes whoever you think you are
and throws you back to what you have
always been

and who is there to listen
how they react with more of it
emitted onto a battlefield of shame
where fears match other fears
and someone must submit,bested or
victorious, horns locked, heads butted

to what karmic end
a display, caveman ancient achieving
what?

look, you have a right to your anger
but it only takes you so far
if you don't use it to do something
it becomes a sore, unhealed
the pain of it lurking under a flap of skin
saps your energy
steals your perspective, alters you
steals your perspective, narrows your view
of, well, everything

you become myopic
pained and generally a
S.O.B

Let go of it, use it,
Redirect its power
Find who you are
There is a better self in there
You can evolve, get on
With life,
Anger will murder you, slowly
But your spirit will die
And the anger will strangle your target
Even as it consumes you inside

Let it go, bro, let it go
And move on
Serenity is more the mark of a
Fully mature man
Than a trail of fuck you, you m…..f..er
And a right cross to some bastards jaw.

Red Bikini, Three Legged Dog

Guy on a scooter screams
"come on, damn it, stop it
Stop the fuckin crying"
To a boy of about 7 or 8
As his Mom coaxes him along a
cement boardwalk, by the sea
the boy cries, loudly until muffled
by his 6 foot three, 250 pound father
as he put his beefy hand across his mouth
and the mother sighs
"let's get a hot dog at the roller coaster"

And a tall black woman bounces her breasts
High and low, syncopated with her running
While she jumps in perfect time with a
boxers jump rope
A vision of grace, across this otherwise coarse
Place, where,thousands, gathered now, across a once abandoned beach
demanded by censors of health, and speech, quiet for now

Two beer bellied men who nail up dry wall
all week, carry a mattress to a favorite spot
for a truck load of family to commence a day

away from hard labor and being pushed around
and they make another trip to transport broken planks
of palettes to fuel the nights fire
a ballet of activity
volleyballers shirtless
women in thongs flying at saves
footballs airborne
Frisbees astray
surfers in bliss away from it all
gliding confidently to shore
not a thought in the way of enjoying
It at all

A guy once young sits
In a wheel chair, with two flags on it
one leg in a prosthetic, and one arm gone
looking out at the bay, with a warriors' smile,
blessing, perhaps, all the red, white and blue
as his girlfriend in a red bikini bottom, and white bra
walks a three legged black lab
a three piece band of guys who live in a nearby condo
all in cowboy hats, play the days tune, "God Bless the USA"
and the boys sing along, the girls cuddle near, July 4th is good this year.

Who Stole the Melting Pot

When optimism was extant
When Americans imagined we were one
When immigrants came from everywhere
When the light of Liberty burned bright
When everyone could recite
"give me your tired your poor
Your huddled masses yearning to breathe free
The wretched refuse of your teaming shore,
Send these the homeless, tempest- tost to me.
I lift my lamp beside the golden door"
Find anyone under 30 who can say it from memory
or know its author or even its meaning back then in
1883

When did it all end?
That we were a cauldron that took in everyone
Melted them together, into an alloy stronger than before
a bouillabaisse of ethnicity, race, culture, sturm und drang,
persecution, upheaval, and ultimately a renewal
here, where for whatever did not reign, for whatever
dream would be delayed or forgotten, often on an uneven
field of play
freedom and liberty reigned

who stole that cauldron, that melting pot
that smelted ancestors and antecedents down
to one cultural,lasting, thing that was America
after all

no more apple pies
picket fences
wild west folklore
universal themes
under big sky's
rising suns revealing spectacular vistas

no more mixing allowed
everyone into their silos of grief and woe
afraid to come out
grief and hurt requiring recompense
unity disallowed
a narrative of separation, reparation
and doubt

Emerson had his say back in the day
1845
"An Asylum of All Nations---
The energy of the Irish, Germans, Swedes,
Poles, Cossacks, and all the European tribes- of the
Africans and of the Polynesians- will construct a new
Race, a new religion, a new state, a new literature, which will
Be as vigorous, as the new Europe that came out of the
Smelting pot of the Dark Ages"

Quaint, perhaps, even utopian
Or rather optimism about what
could be, and millions came to find no
streets of gold, but something more
a place where you could become whatever
it was your destiny required

bring back that smelting pot
find the cauldron that became a
melting pot
renew the metaphor that together
we will emerge stronger and united
and restore the American dream
before
the light of Liberty burns so low
it is extinguished by an ill wind.

End Talks

Always an end to things
only impermanence lasting
pain and joy transitory,
accomplishments forgotten, gains
in retreat, every touch, bruise, scar
tenderness, even all those screams,
apologies, détente's faded
lifetimes captured in the wrinkled brow
now deep crevices on a face in the morning mirror
that rarely smiles

talks that begin in anger
concluding quietly
knowing that it is over
and who will have the courage to say
"it's time to walk away"

Who is such a seer, clairvoyant,
or so wise to see that the end talk
is but a clarion call to better days
once the loss is put into its place and you move
on
not in a cavalier way, just into a space of

what is next, leaving what was, on the floor
with that pile of other discarded notions
of grandeur, wealth, comfort, love and a bag
full of carnal things

end talks are upholstered with cliché
"stay in touch"
"all I know is, say Yes more than No"
"you have so much to give"
"I really thought it was forever"
"It's better this way"
"I hope you find what you're after"
"I know you'll be happier there (with him, her, the job, the city)"
"If you need anything, you know where you can find me"

Words to avoid the hurt
Thoughts to distract from the fear
Doubts come momentarily then remain
What if's, cloud the way to clarity
To grasp is it another transition or milestone
And if that, what's next, a choice to be made
or a wave of uncontrollable forces to ride to another
rocky shore

The Desperate Man

Master's paint themselves
Capture a moment in oil that is exactly who they are
You know the depictions, of Picasso, Gauguin, and
most famously Van Gogh
the most evocative and frightening to me
is Gustave Courbet's
Desperate Man
Eyes wide open, expressing an unexposed horror
Hands running through and pulling at his hair
A man about to scream at the world
To ward off whatever is to come next

At that moment in 1845
Turmoil was ahead, as monarchies held sway
Over millions of those who lived in poverty and
Dread
As he depicted the lunacy of the time that would
Foment revolution across the continent again
to be crushed, and Gustave with his
brushes as his spears to toss into the bloated
corpus of repression

out of his rebellious spirit he painted

workers pulverizing stone, burials of the common man
and then to further enrage the salon seers
nudes of every sort, salacious, serene, seditious
angering the acclaimed who thought they were the
only ones who had a right to decide what is art

and then in a small frame, he depicted L'origine du Monde
a woman nude resplendent of pubic hair and sheet pulled
over a single breast, in 1866, so evocative it would not be in public
exhibited until 1988
and is still banned some places today

always screaming at the wrong
a socialist, and realist undeterred, full of righteousness
and passion, even asking for the Vendome' column remembering
Napoleonic wars to be removed if not destroyed, as it was
during the ill fated Paris Commune
the aging rebel sent to jail and had to repay
the cost of such excess
but painted,none the less,
even if only fruits and flowers
frightened by the world perhaps, fought back with his only weapons
canvas, brush, and oil, and out lasted them all.

Who Do You Think You Are

Anyway.......

Writing a poem a day and
On weekends more
Three or four a day
Do you really believe anyone cares
What you have to say?

Absurd to conjure how an ordinary life
connects to Aristotle, Nietzsche, or Bukowski
Let alone Camus, London, and certainly not
Hemingway

What expectations have you that you can manage the
grand schemes and essential themes
man after finding himself, at a place somewhere in
between heaven and hell, reeling in life's meaning
on a line certain to break
or catching it, only to have it devoured by the sharks

a man of no obvious talent or vices
strong virtues hidden, by a cloak of single minded desire
to put something there, that wasn't a moment before

of your creation, that might resonate even
send a vibration to another, that you, indeed,
existed, at least on all these pages

How could someone, so interior
virulently anti- social, comfortable alone,
pleased to be on long walks and runs, motioning away, rather
than near, not of fear but in search of solace
ruminating, seeking lessons in everything of consequence
and not

as touched by a monarch butterfly on a sunlit branch
as, the laugh of a child tossed airborne by his young father,
the utter transcendent moment of a kiss on a street corner

who do you think you are to capture any of
it
a poet or just a man, declaring with every word
I am here…….

www.ingramcontent.com/pod-product-compliance
Lightning Source LLC
Chambersburg PA
CBHW021422070526
44577CB00001B/9